CHIVALRY

A Gynocentric Tradition

Peter Wright & Paul Elam

First published in February 2019
by Academic Century Press

Introduction

The importance of chivalry is taught to little girls and boys from the start, outlining for them the various rules of male obligation that will guide sexual relations throughout their lifetimes; i.e., males are here to protect and provide for women.

The victories of legendary heroes whose brave deeds are rounded with applause and happily-ever-afters appears to seal the fate of chivalry as the future path of every man.

Those few who do pause to question chivalry's values - its rote expectation of male sacrifice, possibility of danger or injury, impacts on mental health, potential for exploitation and abuse, or the question of valid compensations for ongoing sacrifices - may conclude that it serves as a poor life map, or worse that it amounts to a malignant and toxic form of masculinity.

We often hear the cry go out 'Chivalry is dead,' with descriptions of some man, somewhere, failing in his role of protecting or accommodating women with expected gestures of courtesy. The individual examples of failure are then often extrapolated to men as a class – if one man has failed then surely other men are in danger of doing as he did, falling prey to their selfish indifference and placing the fairer sex in some kind of danger or discomfort.

Despite fears of chivalry failing *en masse*, what we see when we look around at men in our families and wider communities provides a different picture. We see them demonstrating acts of chivalry both big and small, such as paying for dinner and opening doors, or protecting and providing for the fairer sex with acts of altruism. Thus the chivalry-is-dead complaint appears to act more as a ruse, pressuring already-chivalrous men to feel ashamed on behalf of that one man who failed, serving as a warning that they too could become *like him* if they don't shore up their efforts to be good men. If ever there were a narrative that might intensify men's commitment to chivalry, the portrayal of men failing a proverbial damsel in distress appears to be it.

With the discussion narrowed to whether chivalry is alive or dead, society fails to ask more basic questions – such as what is 'chivalry' in the first place? Where did it originate? Is it a sexist or an egalitarian tradition? Only after answering such questions might we be in a position to determine if chivalry *should* live or die, or perhaps whether it should evolve into something else to keep up with the changing times and evolving gender roles.

This book sets out to answer these questions, surveying the evolution of chivalry from its medieval beginnings to when it later branched into two distinct forms; *military chivalry*, and *gynocentric chivalry*. Moreover, while chivalry is frequently studied in terms of its importance to and impact on women, this book takes time to consider men's experience of chivalry as it plays out in both their relationships and in wider society.

The chapters in Section 1 were originally published as separate articles on websites or in journals, and have since been revised for this edition. As they were not intended for collection in one volume there are several repetitions of comments for which I apologize and ask the reader's grace –they are integral to the structure of the articles and for that purpose I have retained them.

I would also like to thank Paul Elam who has donated two superb articles to this volume; Chapter 6. *Chivalry: A Learned Deathwish*, and Chapter 7. *Death By Chivalry: Portland Edition,* illustrating real world examples of chivalric sacrifice which complement the historical overview of the topic. Section 2 provides a limited selection of articles from historical literature that emphasize the gynocentric tradition of chivalry.

Peter Wright – February 2019

TABLE OF CONTENTS

INTRODUCTION

Contemporary Essays

Selection Of Historical Sources

CONTEMPORARY ESSAYS

1. The Birth Of Chivalric Love

Love and war have always been opposed, as we see in our usual phrase 'make love not war' or in the rhetoric of pro and anti-war camps. That the two are mutually exclusive is obvious enough. However, in twelfth century Europe something peculiar happened that ushered in a melding of these two contrary principles. Here the military code of chivalry was mated with the fancies of courtly love to produce a bastard child which we will here call *chivalric love* (today we simply label it 'chivalry'). Prior to this time chivalry always referred to the military code of behaviour –one that varied from country to country– but one which had absolutely nothing to do with romantic love.

What method did twelfth century society use to bring this about? In a word, *shaming*.

The medieval aristocracy began to ramp up the practice of shaming by choosing the worst behaviours of the most unruly males and extrapolating those behaviours to the entire gender. Sound familiar? Knights were particularly singled out –much like today's sporting heroes who display some kind of *faux pas*- to be used as examples of bad male behaviour requiring the remedy of sweeping cultural reform.

During this time of (supposedly) unruly males, uneducated squires were said to ride mangy horses into mess halls, and rude young men diverted eyes from psalters in the very midst of mass. Among the knights and in the atmosphere of tournaments occasional brawls with grisly incidents occurred – a cracked skull, a gouged eye – as the betting progressed and the dice flew. Male attention to clothing and fashion was said to be appalling, with men happy to go about in sheep and fox skins instead of clothes fashioned of rich and precious stuffs, in colours to better suit them in the company of ladies. And perhaps worst of all were their lack of refinement and manners toward women which was considered offensive.

How and by whom was this unruly gender going to be reformed?
One of the first solutions was posed by a French Countess named
Marie. According to historian Amy Kelly, with her male reforming
ideas;

> "Marie organized the rabble of soldiers, fighting-cocks,
> jousters, springers, riding masters, troubadours, Poitevin
> nobles and debutantes, young chatelaines, adolescent princes,
> and infant princesses in the great hall of Poitiers. Of this
> pandemonium the countess fashioned a seemly and elegant
> society, the fame of which spread to the world. Here was a
> woman's assize to draw men from the excitements of the tilt
> and the hunt, from dice and games, to feminine society, an
> assize to outlaw boorishness and compel the tribute of
> adulation to female majesty."[1]

Countess Marie was one among a long line of reformers to help
usher in a gynocentrism whose aim was to convince men of their
shared flaws –essentially to shame them- and to prescribe romantic
love and concomitant worship of females as the remedy. Via this
program romantic love was welded onto the military code and
introduced as a way to tame men's rowdiness and brutality,
something today's traditionalists agree with in their call for men to
adhere to these same male roles established first in medieval Europe.
One of today's authorities on this period describes the training of
knights in her observation, "The rise of courtly love and its
intersection with chivalry in the West are both events of the twelfth
century. The idea that love is ennobling and necessary for the
education of a knight comes out of the lyrics of this period, but also
in the romances of knighthood. Here the truest lovers are now the
best knights."[2]

With romantic love firmly established within the chivalric code we
begin to see the romantic behaviours of soldiers so familiar to us
today; going to fight and die for his Lady, love letters from the front
lines, a crumpled photo of his sweetheart in a uniform pocket. Rather
than for man, king and country it is his love for "her" that now
drives a man's military sacrifice. This is also the reason why today's
movies portraying warzones and carnage always include a hero and
his Lady/Damsel pausing for a passionate tongue kiss while the

bombs explode around them, as if to suggest that all this carnage is for the sake of her and romantic love. Once accepted into the chivalric canon various love "rules" were enforced with military might –by white knights as we call them– and the resulting culture has been unstoppable. To try and stop it brings the wrath of all those white knights who would quickly challenge you to a duel for breaking the new military goal of romantic love.

Prior to the Middle Ages romantic love was usually considered with suspicion and even viewed as a sign of mental instability requiring removal from the source of trouble and perhaps a medical solution. In the context of universally arranged marriages, romantic love, if it was indulged at all, was done so in a discreet and often underground way without the sanction of polite society. This was the situation worldwide until the advent of the European revolution.

The cult of chivalric love took root first among the aristocratic classes and soon after reached the common classes through literature and storytelling. Romance literature in particular. Having germinated initially in Germany and France in the twelfth centuries, the cult spread on the wings of a burgeoning book production industry that would bring the gynocentric revolution to the entire European continent.

When one considers the subjects in these books – Gawain and Guinevere, Tristan and Isolde, heroic male deeds for women, love scandals, courtship, upper-class weddings, adultery, and status – we are reminded immediately of today's women's magazines that spill out of the magazine racks of shops and waiting rooms.

Women's magazines and the omnipresent romance novel –and women's gluttony for them- can be traced back to this early period in which the term *romance* was actually coined. According to Jennifer Wollock, a professor of Literature at Texas University, such literature had a substantial female readership along with mothers reading to their daughters. Wollock states that the continuing popularity of chivalric love stories is also confirmed by the provenance of romance manuscripts and contents of women's libraries of the late Middle Ages.[2]

The three behaviors of chivalric love-code

Keeping with the male side of the equation, the main behaviors prescribed by the code of chivalric love are the doing of romantic deeds, gallantry and vassalage.

Prior to its redeployment in romantic relationships *gallantry* referred to any courageous behaviour, especially in battle. The word can still mean that. However, under the rules of chivalric love it became, according to the Google dictionary definition, "Polite attention or respect given by men to women." Can these two definitions of gallantry be any further apart? Like the contraries of military chivalry vs. chivalric love, these two definitions of gallantry stretch the definition to cover two completely different domains of behaviour. It appears then that women of the time successfully harnessed men's greatest sacrificial behaviours –chivalry and gallantry- to indulge their narcissistic appetites.

A *vassal* is defined as a bondman, a slave, a subordinate or dependent, or a person who entered into a mutual obligation to a lord or monarch in the context of the feudal system in medieval Europe. The obligations often included military support and mutual protection in exchange for certain privileges, usually including the grant of land held as a fiefdom. Vassalage was then utilized as a conceit that Maurice Valency called "the shaping principle of the whole design of courtly love."[3] Whether it was a knight, troubadour, or commoner the vassal-to-woman routine was the order of the day then, exactly as it is today.[4] Poets adopted the terminology of feudalism, declaring themselves the vassal of the lady and addressing her as *midons* (my lord), which was taken as standard flattery of a woman. One particularly striking practice showing an adaption from the feudal model involved the man kneeling on one knee before the woman. By kneeling down in this way he assumes the posture of a vassal. He speaks, pledging his faith, promising, like a liege man, not to offer his services to anyone else. He goes even further: in the manner of a serf, he makes her a gift of his entire person.

Citing evidence of vassalism Amy Kelly writes, "As symbolized on shields and other illustrations that place the knight in the ritual attitude of commendation, kneeling before his lady with his hands folded between hers, homage signified male service, not domination or subordination of the lady, and it signified fidelity, constancy in that service."[5]

In short it was the lover's feudal relationship between vassal and overlord which provided the lover with a model for his humble and servile conduct.[2]

___

The lead actors – then and now

Imagine twelfth century Europe as a great stage performance enacting the themes of chivalric love, one that would become so popular its actors would continue to serve as role models for the global population 800 years later. The lead actors in this medieval play are as follows, accompanied (in brackets) with the titles we apply to those same actors today as they continue this ancient drama:

Courtly Ladies (= Feminists). Feminists today refer to courtly ladies of the late Middle Ages as the first feminists, or *protofeminists*, and as with modern feminists these women enjoyed considerable privilege and means. In the 12th – 14th centuries evidence shows that women began to agitate for increased authority over the 'correct' way for men and women to conduct relationships, with particular emphasis on what they felt were acceptable roles for males in a dignified and civil society. Not surprisingly this was precisely the time when powerful women were able to establish the female-headed 'courts of love' which acted in a comparable way to today's Family Courts in that both arbitrated love disputes between conflicting couples.

Key literature from the period detailing proper etiquette expected in gender relations was commissioned for writing by powerful women (eg. *The Art of Courtly love*) and in some cases was written by women themselves (eg. Christine de Pizan's writings or those of Marie de France). The emerging discourse acted like a drug that promised the introduction of a one-sided power for females over males, and through the dissemination of romance literature that promise rapidly spread to all social classes in the continent. We have been living with the consequences ever since, a revolution far more significant to the history of gender relations than the introduction of the birth control pill and no-fault divorce combined- the latter being mere epiphenomena generated within a larger culture of chivalric love.

The archetypes introduced into society by these high-born ladies are instantly recognizable; the damsel in distress (women as innocent, woman as helpless, women as victim), the princess (women as beautiful, women as narcissistic subject requiring devotion, women as deserving of special privileges), and the high born Ladies (women as morally pure, women as precious, women as superior, women as entitled). These illusions ensured that the attentions of men would be spent attending to women, a program so successful that modern feminists continue to shape today's cultural landscape with the program of their protofeminists forebears. And just like their forebears, feminists continue to use shaming narratives to facilitate their pedestalizing inheritance.

White Knights (= White Knights). We retain this metaphor for such heroic individuals, men who are gallant in so many ways, but mostly the *wrong* ways such as showing-off to undeserving women and concomitantly delighting in competing with and hurting other men. More than any other player in this play, white knights specialize in gallant behaviour for the purpose of impressing and ultimately getting their egos stroked by women.

For these first white knights the tournament, the forerunner to modern sporting tournaments, consisted of chivalrous competitions or fights in the Middle Ages. In these fights knights were only too willing to hurt their fellow men to win the praise of female spectators. The competitors were observed doing battle by women who would throw their garments into the arena where the sportsmen would pick them up and wear pieces of women's clothes -hence the male wearing a particular woman's scarf would represent her in the tournament.

The men were basically fighting for "her" then, just as they did elsewhere on real battlefields for wife and mother. The gallant man who won his tournament was granted an opportunity to dally with the woman whom he represented in the ring. We retain this gynocentric tradition today as golf tournaments, football tournaments, martial arts tournaments and so on, all designed to show male prowess where the winning competitors get to dally with the best ladies.

Other activities of white knights include impressing women with big gestures of protection. For example, the 'Enterprise of the Green Shield with the White Lady' was a chivalric order founded by Jean Le Maingre and twelve knights in 1399 committing themselves to the protection of women. Inspired by the ideal of courtly love, the stated purpose of the order was to guard and defend the honour, estate, goods, reputation, fame and praise of all ladies and damsels, an undertaking that earned the praise of Christine de Pizan. Le Maingre, tired of receiving complaints from ladies, maidens, and widows claiming to be oppressed by powerful men bent on depriving them of the lands and honours, and finding no knight or squire willing to defend their just cause, founded an order of twelve knights sworn to carry "a shield of gold enamelled with green and a white lady inside".

The twelve knights, after swearing this oath, affirmed a long letter explaining their purpose and disseminated it widely in France and beyond her borders. The letter explained that any lady young or old finding herself the victim of injustice could petition one or more or the knights for redress and that knight would respond promptly and leave whatever other task he was performing to fight the lady's oppressor personally. The similarities of this Order with contemporary enterprises such as the White Ribbon Campaign in which male "ambassadors" pledge an oath to all of womanhood to never condone, excuse or remain silent about violence against women, and to intervene and take action against any man accused of wrongdoing against a woman. The similarities in these gallant missions make clear that the lineage of white knights has progressed seamlessly into the modern era.

Troubadours I (= "pick-up artistry" or "game" promoters). The troubadours' job was to spread the word about the virtues of chivalric love through music, song, poetry and storytelling. Aristocracy and commoner alike enjoyed hearing tales about bravery, and ladies were swept away with epic love poems as the troubadours practiced the rituals of chivalric love. Just like PUAs or Gamers today who write and speak in "praise of pussy," troubadours too were composers and promoters of the 'arts of love' aimed at securing sexual fulfilment.

Like those troubadours, Roosh and Roissy (etc.) continue the tradition of prose-writing to illustrate the many ways to flatter women in order to get into their pants. *Game* is a very apt word for this 800 yr old tradition, with its proscription for rehearsed lines and lack of personal authenticity. It is a scripted game of women-worship aimed at a narrow goal. In essence this Casanova routine amounts to a *feigning of chivalric love for the purposes of manipulation*, usually to gain sex. When modern women call these men 'players' they may be very close to the mark. While Roosh et.al. outwardly claim to reject chivalry, they nevertheless embrace its tenets like consummate thespians.

Troubadours II (= Profeminist Men). Unlike the troubadours mentioned above who advocated for a love aimed at sexual fulfilment, Troubadour II advocated a more idealized love of longing that did not consummate in sexual fulfilment. In essence these men more resembled sycophantic Romeos than horny Casanovas. The guiding concept for them was called "fin' amors," which meant pure love. Such men were particularly prevalent in the north of France, whereas in the south we see that troubadours (type I mentioned up above) celebrated a love that was adulterous or carnal in which full sexual encounters were sought.

Another thing that distinguished type II troubadours from the former is authenticity. These men appeared to identify wholly with the role and were not merely players. The desire to serve women as their vassal, or perhaps as their masochistic slave, called upon their innermost character. Think of today's version being the typical profeminist men who work slavishly to pass on the message of their feminist superiors, much as these troubadours slaved to advocate the narcissistic idiosyncrasies of their Ladies. The vassalage role applies here more than with any other character of the Middle Ages – not as a merely pretentious means-to-an-end routine to gain sex, but rather as a soul-affirming act.

––––––

Which brings us to gynocentrism. It is clear from the foregoing that unless evidence of (broadspread) gynocentric culture can be found prior to the Middle Ages, then gynocentrism is precisely 800 years old. In order to determine if this thesis is valid we need first to define exactly what we mean by "gynocentrism".

The term gynocentrism has been in circulation since the 1800's, as far as I can tell, with the general definition being "focused on women; concerned with only women."[6] Adam Kostakis further qualifies gynocentrism as, "male sacrifice for the benefit of women" and "the deference of men to women," and he concludes; "Gynocentrism, whether it went by the name honor, nobility, chivalry, or feminism, its essence has gone unchanged. It remains a peculiarly male duty to help the women onto the lifeboats, while the men themselves face a certain and icy death."[7]

From these definitions we see that gynocentrism could refer to any one female-centered practice in an otherwise androcentric society, or to even a single gynocentric act carried out by one individual. With this broad usage in mind the phrase 'gynocentric culture' proves more precise for the purposes of this essay , which phrase I will define here as *any culture instituting rules for gender relationships that benefit females at the expense of males across a broad range of measures.*

At the base of our current form of gynocentrism lies the practice of enforced male sacrifice for the benefit of women. If we accept this definition we need to look back and ask the accompanying question of whether male sacrifices throughout history were always made for the sake of women, or alternatively for the sake of some other primary goal? For instance, when men went to die in vast numbers in wars, was it for women, or was it rather for Man, King and Country? If the latter we cannot then claim that this was a result of some intentional gynocentric culture, at least not in the way I have defined it here. If the sacrifice isn't intended for the benefit women, even if women were occasional beneficiaries of male sacrifice, then we are not dealing with gynocentrism.

Male disposability strictly "for the benefit of women" comes in strongly only after the advent of the 12th century gender revolution in Europe – a revolution that delivered us terms like gallantry, chivalry, chivalric love, courtesy, romance and so on. From that period onward gynocentric practices grew exponentially, culminating in the demands of today's feminism. In sum, gynocentrism was a patchy phenomenon at best before the middle ages, after which it became ubiquitous.

With all this in mind it makes little sense to talk of gynocentric culture starting with the industrial revolution a mere 200 years ago (or 100 or even 30 yrs ago), or of it being two million years old as some would argue. We are not simply fighting two million years of genetic programming; our culturally constructed enemy is much, *much* simpler to pinpoint and to potentially reverse. The historical evidence is strong. All we need do now is look at the circumstances under which gynocentrism first began to flourish and attempt to reverse those circumstances. Specifically, if gynocentric culture was brought about by the practice of shaming, then that is the enemy to target in order to reverse the entire enterprise. For me that process could begin by rejecting the fake moral purity to which women of the last millennia have pretended and against which the worst examples of men have been measured in order to shame the entire gender.

References

1. Amy Kelly, 'Eleanor of Aquitaine and Her Courts of Love'
Source: Speculum, Vol. 12, No. 1 (Published by Medieval Academy
of America, 1937)
2. Jennifer G. Wollock, Rethinking Chivalry and Courtly Love,
(Published by Praeger, 2011)
3. Maurice Valency, In Praise of Love: An Introduction to the Love
Poetry of the Renaissance, (Macmillan, 1961)
4. For an excellent article about vassaldom today see Gordon
Wadsworth's 'The Western Butler and his Manhood' which
indicates an unbroken line between the romantic vassaldom of the
Middle Ages and the "butler" role expected of males today.
(Published on AVfM, 2013)
5. Amy Kelly, 'Did Women Have a Renaissance?' in Women,
History, and Theory (Published by UCP Press, 1984)
6. Dictionary.com – Gynocentric
7. Adam Kostakis, Gynocentrism Theory – (Published online, 2011).
Although Kostakis assumes gynocentrism has been around
throughout recorded history, he singles out the Middle Ages for
comment: *"There is an enormous amount of continuity between the
chivalric class code which arose in the Middle Ages and modern
feminism... One could say that they are the same entity, which now
exists in a more mature form – certainly, we are not dealing with two
separate creatures."*

2. A Bastardized Chivalry

> "Chivalry, as understood by Modern Sentimental Feminism, means unlimited licence for women in their relations with men, and unlimited coercion for men in their relations with women. To men all duties and no rights, to women all rights and no duties, is the basic principle underlying Modern Feminism, Suffragism, and the bastard chivalry it is so fond of invoking." – (Bax, 1913, p. 141)

In 1913 English barrister Ernest B. Bax observed that chivalry had undergone an alteration or, as he understood it, a corruption from its earlier intent of *deference to weakness*. (Bax, 1913). He contended that the original definition was no longer current since in its modern application the question of a person's sex took precedence over that of weakness proper. Instead of chivalry being directed to the care and protection of children, frail elders, the disabled, or the wounded in battle as in earlier times, Bax understood the new chivalry as being confined strictly to "sex privilege and sex favouritism pure and simple." (Bax, 1913, p. 100).

The claim of chivalry being redirected along predominantly sexual lines is confirmed by most modern dictionaries, for example in the Cambridge Dictionary which defines it as 'Very polite, honest, and kind behaviour, especially toward women.' (Dictionary C, 2015). Following in the footsteps of Bax the following essay will explore the gendered facets of "bastard chivalry," focusing on its promotion of sex-favouritism and associated impacts on male health.

<u>The emergence and divergence of 'two chivalries'</u>

The earliest meaning of chivalry referred to a code of behaviour followed by medieval knights of Europe, the word itself being derived from Old French *chevalerie*, from medieval Latin *caballerius* meaning 'horseman' (Dictionary O.E., 2008). As Bax observes;

"The term meant originally the virtues associated with knighthood considered as a whole, bravery even to the extent of reckless daring, loyalty to the chief or feudal superior, generosity to a fallen foe, general open-handedness, and open-heartedness, including, of course, the succour of the weak and the oppressed generally, *inter alia*, the female sex when in difficulties… [O]nly a fragment of the original connotation of the word chivalry is covered by the term as used in our time, and that even that fragment is torn from its original connection and is made to serve as a scarecrow in the field of public opinion to intimidate all who refuse to act upon, or who protest against, the privileges and immunities of the female sex." (Bax, 1913, pp. 100-101)

The variation referred to by Bax can be traced back to an emerging culture of courtly love and its harnessing of chivalry to new ends, which in the West is a development of the twelfth century. According to historian Jennifer G. Wollock of Texas University, "the idea that love is ennobling and necessary for the education of a knight comes out of the lyrics of this period, but also in the romances of knighthood. Here the truest lovers are now the best knights." (Wollock, 2011, p. 42)

In that historical context chivalry was subjected to a new contextual application, taken up by an emerging culture of courtly love in which men were taught to direct their chivalric cares, concern, protection, obedience, and service exclusively to women (Alfonsi, 1986). Over the course of two centuries there emerged two distinctly differentiated versions of chivalry: a continuing *military chivalry* with its code of conduct and proper contexts, and a *romantic chivalry* complete with its code of conduct and proper contexts.

It is difficult to pinpoint when the culture of romantic chivalry constellated and found relative independence from its military forerunner, but the evidence of troubadour poetry, romance fiction (Yalom, 2012), and etiquette manuals (Cappelanus, 1990) detailing the elaborate conventions of romantic chivalry attest to its emergence by the end of the twelfth century. Central to that revolution was the imperial patronage of Eleanor of Aquitaine and her daughter Marie de Champagne who together elaborated the military notion of chivalry into one of servicing ladies.

Prior to the twelfth century romantic chivalry did not exist as a gendered construct; it was in the Middle Ages that it developed cultural complexity and became the enduring cultural norm we inherit today. The following timeline details the birth of romantic chivalry along with significant historical events that promoted its survival:

1102 AD: Romantic chivalry first introduced

William IX, Duke of Aquitaine, the most powerful feudal lord in France, wrote the first troubadour poems and is widely considered the first troubadour. Parting with the tradition of fighting wars strictly on behalf of man, king, God and country, William is said to have had the image of his mistress painted on his shield, whom he called *midons* (my Lord) saying that it was his will to bear her in battle, as she had borne him in bed.

1152 AD: Queen Eleanor of Aquitaine invites poet Bernard de Ventadorn to compose songs of love for her and her husband, Henry II. The songs lay down a code of chivalric behaviour for how a good man should treat his "lady," which Eleanor employs in an apparent attempt to civilize her husband and his male associates. Eleanor and other noblewomen began to encourage poetic narratives that set expectations on how men should act around them (School of Life, 2011).

1168 – 1198 AD: The romantic chivalry trope is elaborated and given imperial patronage by Eleanor and her daughter Marie. At Eleanor's court in Poitiers Eleanor and Marie embroidered the Christian military code of chivalry with a code for romantic lovers, thus putting women at the center of courtly life – and in doing so they had permanently changed the face of chivalry (McKnight, 1994).

Key events:

1170 AD: Eleanor and Marie established the formal Courts of Love presided over by themselves and a jury of 60 noble ladies who would investigate and hand down judgements on love-disputes according to the newly introduced code governing gender relations. The courts were modelled precisely along the lines of the traditional feudal courts where disputes between retainers had been settled by the powerful lord. In this case however the disputes were between lovers (McKnight, 1994).

1180 AD: Marie directs Chrétien de Troyes to write *Lancelot, the Knight of the Cart*, a love story about Lancelot and Guinevere elaborating the nature of romantic chivalry. Chrétien de Troyes objected to the implicit approval of the adulterous affair between Lancelot and Guinevere that Marie had directed him to write about and failed to finish it, but later poets completed the story on Chrétien's behalf. Chrétien also wrote other famous romances including *Erec and Enide* (McKnight, 1994).

1188 AD: Marie directs her chaplain Andreas Capellanus to write *The Art of Courtly Love*. This guide to the chivalric codes of romantic love is a document that could pass as contemporary in almost every respect, excepting for the outdated class structures and assumptions. Many of the admonitions in Andreas textbook are believed to have come from the women who directed the writing (McKnight, 1994).

1180 – 1380 AD: In two hundred years the culture or romantic chivalry spread from France to become instituted in all the principle courts of Europe, and went on to capture the imagination of men, women and children of all social classes. According to Jennifer Wollock (2011), the continuing popularity of chivalric love stories is confirmed by the contents of women's libraries of the late Middle Ages, literature which had a substantial female readership including mothers reading to their daughters. Aside from the growing access to literature, chivalric culture values spread via everyday interactions among people in which they shared the ideas.

The aristocratic classes who first developed the romantic chivalry trope did not exist in a vacuum. The courtly themes they enacted would most certainly have captured the imaginations of the lower classes though public displays of pomp and pageantry, troubadours and tournaments, minstrels and playwrights, the telling of romantic stories, and of course the gossip flowing everywhere which would have exerted a powerful effect on the peasant imagination (Wright 2014).

It is possible that those of even lower classes adopted some assumptions portrayed in the public displays, such as the importance of chivalrous behavior toward women and perhaps a belief in women's purity and moral superiority. Certainly by the 1600s and beyond, the adaptation of romantic chivalry by lower classes was in full career, as evidenced by Lucrezia Marinella who provides an example of Venetian society from the year 1600:

> It is a marvelous sight in our city to see the wife of a shoemaker or butcher or even a porter all dressed up with gold chains round her neck, with pearls and valuable rings on her fingers, accompanied by a pair of women on either side to assist her and give her a hand, and then, by contrast, to see her husband cutting up meat all soiled with ox's blood and down at heel, or loaded up like a beast of burden dressed in rough cloth, as porters are.

> At first it may seem an astonishing anomaly to see the wife dressed like a lady and the husband so basely that he often appears to be her servant or butler, but if we consider the matter properly, we find it reasonable because it is necessary for a woman, even if she is humble and low, to be ornamented in this way because of her natural dignity and excellence, and for the man to be less so, like a servant or beast born to serve her.

> Women have been honored by men with great and eminent titles that are used by them continually, being commonly

referred to as *donne*, for the name *donna* means lady and mistress. When men refer to women thus, they honor them, though they may not intend to, by calling them ladies, even if they are humble and of a lowly disposition. In truth, to express the nobility of this sex men could not find a more appropriate and fitting name than *donna*, which immediately shows women's superiority and precedence over men, because by calling women mistress they [men] show themselves of necessity to be subjects and servants (Marinella, 1999).

While popular recognition of the 'two chivalries' ran concurrently over several hundred years, the notion of military chivalry would eventually be relegated to obscurity in popular discourse as described in the observations above by Bax and evidenced by definitions in modern dictionaries.

<u>Ideological structure of romantic chivalry</u>

Romantic chivalry is alluded to by alternative terms such as benevolent sexism, romantic love, gentlemanliness, courtesy, gallantry, heroism, or simply chivalry. The practice has roots in what some scholars have referred to as chivalric 'love service,' (Bennett, 2013) a ritualized form of devotion by men toward women popularized by troubadours in the Middle Ages. The earliest conceptualization of love service borrowed from the vocabulary of medieval feudalism, mimicking ties between a liegeman and his overlord; i.e., the male lover is referred to as *homo ligius* (the woman's liegeman, or 'my man') who pledged *honor*, and *servitium* (service) to the lady via a posture of feudal homage. The lady was addressed as *midons* (literally 'my lord'), and also by *dominus* (denoting the feudal Lady) (Alfonsi, 1986). These practices form the ideological taproot of modern romantic chivalry.

The conventions and indeed the lived practices of romantic chivalry celebrated first among the upper classes made their way by degrees eventually to the middle classes and finally to the lower classes – or rather they broke class structure altogether in the sense that all Western peoples became inheritors of the customs regardless of their social station. Today chivalry is a norm observed across the majority of global cultures, an explicitly gynocentric norm aimed to increase the comfort, safety and power of women, while affording men a sense of purpose and occasional heroism in addressing that same task (Wright, 2014).

C.S. Lewis referred to the growth of romantic chivalry as "the feudalisation of love," (Lewis, 2013, p. 2) making the observation that it has left no corner of our ethics, our imagination, or our daily life untouched. He observed that European society has moved essentially from a social feudalism, involving a contractual arrangement between a feudal lord and his vassal, to a *sexual feudalism* involving a comparable contract between men and women as symbolized in the act of a man going down on one knee to propose marriage (Wright, 2014).

<u>Education in chivalry through the use of shame</u>

The education and transmission of chivalry from generation to generation is overseen by parents, teachers and peers, and is reinforced by a plethora of culture-mediums including social media, mainstream media, political narratives, romance novels, music, cinema and the arts. Through these mediums romantic chivalry is internalized by young girls and boys as models of expected gendered behaviour.

An early example appears in the 1825 volume *The History of Chivalry or Knighthood and Its Times*, describing the education of a boy in the expectations of romantic chivalry. The author tells that in Medieval Europe the intellectual and moral education of boys in the chivalric code was given by the time they turned seven years by the ladies of the court:

> "From the lips of the ladies the gentle page learned both his catechism and the art of love, and as the religion of the day was full of symbols, and addressed to the senses, so the other feature of his devotion was not to be nourished by abstract contemplation alone. He was directed to regard some one lady of the court as the type of his heart's future mistress; she was the centre of all his hopes and wishes; to her he was obedient, faithful, and courteous." (Mills, 1825, pp. 32-33)

To illustrate such education we are provided an anecdote of a young boy named Jean de Saintre, page of honour at the court of the French king. A Dame des Belles Cousines enquired of the boy 'the name of the mistress of his heart's affections':

> The simple youth replied, that he loved his lady mother, and next to her, his sister Jacqueline was dear to him. "Young man," rejoined the lady, "I am not speaking of the affection due to your mother and sister; but I wish to know the name of the lady to whom you are attached *par amours*." The poor boy was still more confused, and he could only reply that he loved no one *par amours*.
>
> The Dame des Belles Cousines charged him with being a traitor to the laws of chivalry, and declared that his craven spirit was evinced by such an avowal. "Whence," she enquired, "sprang the valiancy and knightly feats of Launcelot, Gawain, Tristram, Giron the courteous, and other ornaments of the round table of Ponthus, and of those knights and squires of this country whom I could enumerate: whence the grandeur of many whom I have known to arise to renown, except from the noble desire of maintaining themselves in the grace and esteem of the ladies; without which spirit-stirring sentiment they must have ever remained in the shades of obscurity? And do you, coward valet, presume to declare that you possess no sovereign lady, and desire to have none?"
>
> Jean underwent a long scene of persecution on account of his confession of the want of proper chivalric sentiment, but he was at length restored to favour by the intercession of the ladies of the court. He then named as his mistress Matheline de Coucy, a child only ten years old. (Mills, 1825, pp. 32-33)

The pressure applied to the boy of this account, including shaming responses for his non-conformity, provide testament to the pressures that accompanied, and continue to accompany, deviance from the dictates of romantic chivalry. Education of this kind is common on social media today where read commentaries about "unchivalrous" males who by their failures become the subject of mockery and shame (a Google search for *unchivalrous* co-occurs with the word 'shame' 54,900 times; 'ashamed' 23,400; 'pathetic' 31,000; 'loser' 14,500; and 'unmanly' 9,960 times respectively). (Google, 2018)

A recent example of a shaming narrative serving as an educative prompt appeared in the online *Conservative Woman* (Perrins, 2018). The article recounted an incident from the year 1989 when 25-year-old gunman Marc Lépine entered the École Polytechnique armed with a semi-automatic rifle and ordered the males and females to form into separate groups. He then began killing several women and injuring some of the men. The author lamented that these men "abandoned" the women in an "act of abdication" that would have been unthinkable in previous, more chivalric periods of history. The author admits she was "pretty shocked that the men left," and finally blames "the collapse of protective masculinity" as a preventable factor in the deaths of those women.

Regarding younger children, a search for chivalry and related terms such as "knight" "damsel in distress" and "princess" in the children's section of Amazon Books website (for ages 2–12) generated over 10,000 results, revealing that a fascination with medieval gender roles remains popular with children and their parents today, a result that can be multiplied with the addition of teenage and adult books in the same genre (Amazon, 2018). One example titled *Noisy Knights* (for boys aged 2-5) shows pictures of a distressed damsel menaced by a fire-breathing dragon (the book includes a battery operated button to make her scream in audio) (Taplin, 2010). The text asks the reader if he knows of any knight who might be brave enough to save her, a question clearly designed to lead young male reader to volunteer service, imagining himself stepping into a position of danger to protect the damsel and reduce her distress.

Romantic chivalry is further popularized in video games and Disney movies, for example, which are bestsellers among children in the digital age. Many themes of romantic chivalry appear charming in isolation from their real-world implications, a delight to the imagination, however as the field of narrative psychology likes to remind; our identities consist of such stuff as dreams are made. The stories that children and adults absorb are the stories they *enact*, and in this case there is potential for men and boys to enact them to the neglect of their health, safety, dignity and larger human potential (Wright & Elam, 2017, p. 29-31).

<u>Benevolent Sexism</u>

In the field of sociology chivalry remains a much-researched topic, though renamed and problematized under the heading 'benevolent sexism.' According to P. Glick *et.al* (2000), the attitudes tapped in the Benevolent Sexism Scale are closer to medieval ideologies of chivalry than they are to other modern social or political movements. Benevolent Sexism (often shortened humorously to 'BS') is rooted in the traditional culture-structures guiding personal relationships between men and women and is not an outcome of contemporary politics, even when reinforced by political discourse and encoded in legislation (Glick, *et.al.*, 2000).

Benevolent sexism is described as the expression of reverence and care toward women while promising they will be protected and provided for by men, and is thus experienced subjectively by women as an agreeable form of sexism (Hammond, *et.al.*, 2014). Moreover, research has shown that these attitudes objectively *do* benefit women because men who express agreement with benevolent sexism are generally more caring, satisfying, and positive relationship partners (Hammond, *et.al.*, 2014).

In their study aptly titled *The Allure of Sexism*, Matthew D. Hammond *et.al.* (2014) researched whether a sense of entitlement to special treatments—a central facet of narcissism based on feelings of superiority and deservingness—was linked with endorsement of benevolent sexism by women across time:

> 'If women endorse benevolent sexism because of the individual-level benefits it offers, then women's endorsement of benevolent sexism should vary depending on dispositional differences in psychological entitlement. Psychological entitlement is a core facet of narcissism, which encompasses feelings that the self deserves nice things, social status and praise, and beliefs of the self as superior, highly intelligent, and attractive (Campbell, Bonacci, Shelton, Exline & Bushman, 2004; Campbell, Brunell, & Finkel, 2006; Emmons, 1987; Miller & Campbell, 2010). The model of narcissistic self-regulation characterizes psychological entitlement as manifesting in efforts to gain esteem, status, and resources (Campbell & Foster, 2007; Campbell et al., 2006; Morf & Rhodewalt, 2001). Such efforts include adopting a superficially charming, confident, and energetic approach to social interactions (Foster, Shrira, & Campbell, 2006; Paulhus, 1998), taking personal responsibility for successes and attributing failures to external sources (Chowning & Campbell, 2009; Rhodewalt & Morf, 1998), and acting selfishly to secure material gains even when it means exploiting others (Campbell et al., 2004; Campbell, Bush, Brunell, & Shelton, 2005).' (Hammond, *et.al.*, 2014, p. 2).

Perhaps unsurprisingly, the study found that a psychological sense of entitlement in women does mediate endorsement of benevolent sexism. Moreover, the researchers theorized that characteristics of narcissistic entitlement – those which drive resource-attainment and self-enhancement strategies – are the same qualities that promote women's adoption of benevolent sexism:

'First, benevolent sexism facilitates the capacity to gain material resources and complements feelings of deservingness by promoting a structure of intimate relationships in which men use their access to social power and status to provide for women (Chen et al., 2009). Second, benevolent sexism reinforces beliefs of superiority by expressing praise and reverence of women, emphasizing qualities of purity, morality, and culture which make women the ''fairer sex.'' Indeed, identifying with these kinds of gender-related beliefs (e.g., women are warm) fosters a more positive self-concept (Rudman, Greenwald, & McGhee, 2001).

Moreover, for women higher in psychological entitlement, benevolent sexism legitimizes a self-centric approach to relationships by emphasizing women's special status within the intimate domain and men's responsibilities of providing and caring for women. Such care involves everyday chivalrous behaviors, such as paying on a first date and opening doors for women (Sarlet et al., 2012; Viki et al., 2003), to more overarching prescriptions for men's behavior toward women, such as being ''willing to sacrifice their own well-being'' to provide for women and to ensure women's happiness by placing her ''on a pedestal'' (Ambivalent Sexism Inventory; Glick & Fiske, 1996). Thus, women higher in psychological entitlement should be particularly enticed by benevolent sexism because it justifies provision and praise from men as expected behavior and does not require women to reciprocate the reverence or material gains, which men provide.' (Hammond, *et.al.*, 2014, pp. 3-4).

While the Hammond study describes the sense of entitlement by women in terms of narcissistic motivation, it is more accurately termed *gynocentric* based on the exclusively gendered context, i.e. woman as center of the relational contract who feels deserving of benevolent gestures from men and boys. While deservingness is an integral feature of narcissism, the concept of *gynocentrism* provides more specificity than does narcissism because women may not feel entitled, for example, to special treatment by non-intimate males nor by other women (as compared to an individual scoring high on standard narcissism scales), reserving instead the sense of entitlement for intimate gendered relationships. The gendered context of women's sense of entitlement is confirmed by studies showing that women tend to score lower than men on global narcissism scales (Grijalva, *et.al.,* 2013), however such measures fail to take into account the exclusively gendered domain in which benevolent sexism operates and in which the level of female narcissism may be much higher.

A 2018 survey of 782 female subjects found women believe male partners displaying benevolent sexist attitudes are more willing to protect, provide for, and commit to them, which in turn rendered those men more attractive. Interestingly, feminist women were just as likely as non-feminist women to prefer benevolently sexist men over more egalitarian men regardless of whether they rated themselves as high or low feminists. High feminists rated the benevolent sexist men as more patronizing and undermining than did low feminists, but felt the positive sides of benevolent sexism outweighed the negatives (Gul & Kupfer, 2018).

Societal chivalry

Beyond the relational sphere, chivalric customs are utilized to facilitate more empowerment of women via the initiatives of national and international governing bodies. This can be witnessed for example in anti-violence campaigns such as the White Ribbon initiative in Australia which asks men to "Stand up, speak out, *and act*" to ensure the dignity, safety and comfort of any women, even strangers, who might find themselves in real or imagined danger (Seymour, 2018).

We witness it again internationally in the HeForShe campaign initiated by UN Women Ambassador Emma Watson, who in her introductory speech appealed to feminist oversight of gendered matters six times, and then to the importance of men offering their chivalric support to women's empowerment: "I want men to take up this mantle. So their daughters, sisters and mothers can be free from prejudice… I am inviting you to step forward, to be seen to speak up, to be the 'he' for 'she.' And to ask yourself if not me, who? If not now, when?" (Watson, 2014).

Chivalry operates outside the interpersonal sphere in which men have traditionally given up their seats in buses, whereby governments are now providing seats for women in legislative assemblies and in boardrooms via quotas. Similarly the act of a man opening a door for a woman is now enacted by governments who open doors for women into universities and workforces via the practice of affirmative action (Wright, 2017). Indeed chivalry has arguably been exploited to meet objectives of women's empowerment since at least the time of Bax, who in the year 1887 contended that "It is all very well to say they [feminists] repudiate chivalry. They are ready enough to invoke it politically when they want to get a law passed in their favour – while socially, to my certain knowledge, many of them claim it as a right every whit as much as ordinary women." (Bax, 1887, p. 114-121).

<u>Negative health outcomes for men and boys</u>

Men and boys who enact chivalric masculinity may pay a considerable price in the process, psychologically, socially or physically. Romantic chivalry emphasizes protection of women (Dictionary Y, 2018), thus men are placed in danger of being injured, maimed or killed when "intervening" in difficult situations such as those evoked by the White Ribbon initiatives, or while working in the male dominated professions of military, police, and firefighters for whom acts of benevolent sexism are celebrated.

The masculine norm of stoicism (Murray, *et.al.,* 2008) involving the repression of emotion and the cultivation of indifference to pleasure or pain serves maintain men's chivalric focus on women's assumed need for support, protection and male deference. Conversely, if a man or boy becomes focused on his own emotions, pain, pleasure or needs, he risks being viewed as a poor protector and provider (i.e. less chivalrous), which will be likely met with social shaming if not outright violence as modes of punishing transgressions and encouraging compliance.

The gendered morality of chivalry dictates that men and boys receive less compassion and assistance than their female counterparts (Eagly & Crowley, 1986), are more likely to be viewed as suitable targets for infliction of violence, pain and other harm (Feldman-Hall, *et.al.*, 2016), are more likely to receive harsher legal penalties than women for offenses (Curry, *et.al.*, 2004), and conversely perpetrators of crime *against* males are more likely to receive lenient sentences as compared to those who perpetrate crimes against women who receive the longest sentences (Curry, *et.al.*, 2004). Males who suffer disability or mental illness are more often stigmatized and treated with less 'chivalric' compassion or positivity than their female counterparts (Whitley, *et.al.*, 2015). The differential gender outcomes in these examples demonstrate that romantic chivalry fosters a 'sympathy-deficit' toward males and their issues, and a conversely heightened concern for women's issues. This gender-preferential bias has been referred to as *gynosympathy* (Wright, 2016), a practice that negatively impacts men's willingness to seek help and assistance when needed (Eagly & Crowley, 1986).

The employment of traditional sex-role strategies (inclusive of stoicism and chivalry) increase the likelihood of male depression (Addis, 2008; Batty, 2006, Liljegren, 2010, Oliffe, & Phillips, 2008), anxiety, stress, and poorer health behaviors (Eisler, *et.al.*, 1998), suicide (Houle, *et.al.*, 2008), and accidental death (Stillion & McDowell, 2002), however the precise degree to which chivalry contributes to these outcomes requires further research.

<u>Summary and conclusion</u>

The chivalry surveyed in this essay is both sexist and gynocentric in nature, one that demands men provide numerous psychological gratifications and material benefits to recipient women. Enactment of chivalric behaviours may also provide secondary benefits for men and boys, such as increased social/peer approval and greater access to female romantic partners (Hammond, *et.al.*, 2014). The chivalric role offers heterosexual men a life-map to guide their social behaviour while providing a sense of self based on service to women. This in contrast to socially disapproved identities such as 'unchivalrous' males, voluntarily confirmed bachelors (Holland, 1959), or alternatively to gay or transgender men whose identities are not built on service to women (Polimeni, *et.al.*, 2000; Nagoshi, *et.al.*, 2008).

Men adhering to chivalric behaviour are rewarded with social valorization, and in the more extreme examples are praised as selfless "heroes" for which medals are awarded by mainstream social institutions. On the negative side of the equation there may be a lack of recognition for ongoing sacrifices – chivalry as rote expectation, an assigned role, codified and reinforced with shame. In both adhering, and in failing to adhere to the dictates of romantic chivalry, the cumulative psychosocial burden on men may be considerable – including negative mental and physical health impacts as outlined above.

In an age of equality one might ask what continuing relevance has romantic chivalry? If we follow the definition of chivalry in the Cambridge Dictionary as a "very polite, honest, and kind behaviour," is it still necessary to add the usual adjunct "…especially by men toward women"? Omission of the gendered framing shifts the emphasis toward extending a universal politeness, honesty, and kindness toward all peoples, reviving the older sense of chivalry from which romantic chivalry originally diverged to become the dominant or "bastardized" meaning.

Such an amendment would free men and boys to discover a variety of non-gynocentric masculinities, and revive the notion of 'common courtesy' as a basis for reciprocal service and devotion between men and women. Mainstream commenters occasionally pay lip service to the idea of de-genderizing chivalry (Waldman, 2013), but until such time as that sentiment is actualized in popular culture we might conclude with a rephrasing of Emma Watson's HeForShe proposition and ask; "I am inviting you to step forward, to be seen to speak up, to be the "we" for "all." And to ask yourself if not me, who? If not now, when?"

References

Addis, M. E. (2008). Gender and depression in men. *Clinical Psychology: Science and Practice, 15*(3), 153-168.
Alfonsi, S. R. (1986). *Masculine submission in troubadour lyric* (Vol. 34). Peter Lang Pub Inc.
Amazon. (2018, September 9). https://www.amazon.com/

Batty, Z. (2006). Masculinity and depression: Men's subjective experience of depression, coping and preferences for therapy and gender role conflict.

Bax, E. B. (1887). No Misogyny but true Equality. *To-day: monthly magazine of scientific socialism*, (47), 114-121.

Bax, E. B. (1913). *The Fraud of Feminism* (p. 141). Grant Richards.

Bennett, J. M., & Karras, R. M. (Eds.). (2013). Chivalry and Love Service. In *The Oxford handbook of women and gender in medieval Europe*. Oxford University Press.

Capellanus, A. (1990). *The Art of Courtly Love* (Vol. 33). Columbia University Press.

Curry, T. R., Lee, G., & Rodriguez, S. F. (2004). Does victim gender increase sentence severity? Further explorations of gender dynamics and sentencing outcomes. *Crime & Delinquency*, *50*(3), 319-343.

Dictionary, C. (2015). Cambridge dictionaries online.

Dictionary, O. E. (2008). Oxford english dictionary. *Retrieved May*, *30*, 2008.

Dictionary, Y. nd 15 April 2015. [Definition: Chivalry is defined as a quality held by knights and gentlemen offering courage, honor and protection to women. *A man who stands in front of his wife and child during a robbery is an example of chivalry.*]

Eagly, A. H., & Crowley, M. (1986). Gender and helping-behavior— A meta-analytic review of the social psychological literature. Psychological Bulletin, 100, 283–308.

Eisler, R. M., Skidmore, J. R., & Ward, C. H. (1988). Masculine gender-role stress: Predictor of anger, anxiety, and health-risk behaviors. *Journal of Personality Assessment*, *52*(1), 133-141.

FeldmanHall, O., Dalgleish, T., Evans, D., Navrady, L., Tedeschi, E., & Mobbs, D. (2016). Moral chivalry: Gender and harm sensitivity predict costly altruism. *Social psychological and personality science*, *7*(6), 542-551.

Glick, P., Fiske, S. T., Mladinic, A., Saiz, J. L., Abrams, D., Masser, B., ... & Annetje, B. (2000). Beyond prejudice as simple antipathy: hostile and benevolent sexism across cultures. *Journal of personality and social psychology*, 79(5), 763.

Google. (2018, September 9). https://www.google.com

Grijalva, E., Newman, D. A., Tay, L., Donnellan, M. B., Harms, P. D., Robins, R. W., & Yan, T. (2015). Gender differences in narcissism: A meta-analytic review. *Psychological bulletin*, *141*(2), 261.

Gul, P., & Kupfer, T. R. (2018). Benevolent Sexism and Mate Preferences: Why Do Women Prefer Benevolent Men Despite Recognizing That They Can Be Undermining?. *Personality and Social Psychology Bulletin*, 0146167218781000.

Hammond, M. D., Sibley, C. G., & Overall, N. C. (2014). The allure of sexism: Psychological entitlement fosters women's endorsement of benevolent sexism over time. Social Psychological and Personality Science, 5(4), 422-429.

Holland, H. (Ed.). (1949). *Why are You Single?*. Farrar, Straus.

Houle, J., Mishara, B. L., & Chagnon, F. (2008). An empirical test of a mediation model of the impact of the traditional male gender role on suicidal behavior in men. *Journal of affective disorders, 107*(1-3), 37-43.

Lewis, C. S. (2013). *The allegory of love.* Cambridge University Press. (p. 2)

Liljegren, T. (2010). The Male Gender Role and Depression.

Marinella, L. (1999). The Nobility and Excellence of Women, and the Defects and Vices of Men, ed. and trans. *Anne Dunhill (Chicago and London: University of Chicago Press, 1999)*.

McKnight, C. J. (1994). *Chivalry: The Path of Love*. Chronicle Books Llc.

Mills, C. (1825). *The History of Chivalry or Knighthood and Its Times*. (pp. 32-33) Longman, Hurst, Rees, Orme , Brown and Green.

Murray, G., Judd, F., Jackson, H., Fraser, C., Komiti, A., Pattison, P., ... & Robins, G. (2008). Big boys don't cry: An investigation of stoicism and its mental health outcomes. *Personality and Individual Differences, 44*(6), 1369-1381.

Nagoshi, J. L., Adams, K. A., Terrell, H. K., Hill, E. D., Brzuzy, S., & Nagoshi, C. T. (2008). Gender differences in correlates of homophobia and transphobia. *Sex roles, 59*(7-8), 521.

Oliffe, J. L., & Phillips, M. J. (2008). Men, depression and masculinities: A review and recommendations. *Journal of Men's Health, 5*(3), 194-202.

Perrins, L. (2018, August 11). *No time for heroes: the men who stood by as a maniac shot their female classmate.* Retrieved from https://www.conservativewoman.co.uk/no-time-for-heroes-the-men-who-stood-by-as-a-maniac-shot-their-female-classmates/

Polimeni, A. M., Hardie, E., & Buzwell, S. (2000). Homophobia among Australian heterosexuals: The role of sex, gender role ideology, and gender role traits. *Current Research in Social Psychology, 5*(4), 47-62.

Seymour, K. (2018). "Stand up, speak out and act": A critical reading of Australia's White Ribbon campaign. *Australian & New Zealand Journal of Criminology, 51*(2), 293-310.

Stillion, J. M., & McDowell, E. E. (2002). The early demise of the "stronger" sex: Gender-related causes of sex differences in longevity. *OMEGA-Journal of Death and Dying, 44*(4), 301-318.

Taplin, S. (2010) *Noisy Knights*. Usborne

The School of Life. (2018, August 20) The History of Ideas: Manners. Retrieved from https://youtu.be/JCTzbc76WXY

Waldman, Katy. (August, 2013). *Toward Pan-Chivalry: A New World Order*. Slate.com

Whitley, R., Adeponle, A., & Miller, A. R. (2015). Comparing gendered and generic representations of mental illness in Canadian newspapers: an exploration of the chivalry hypothesis. *Social psychiatry and psychiatric epidemiology*, 50(2), 325-333.

Watson, E. (2014). Gender equality is your issue too. *Speech by UN Women Goodwill Ambassador Emma Watson at a Special Event for the HeForShe Campaign, United Nations Headquarters, New York, 20.*

Wright, P. (2014). *Gynocentrism: From Feudalism to The Modern Disney Princess*. Academic Century Press.

Wright, P. What Ever Happened To Chivalry? In *A Brief History of The Men's Rights Movement: From 1856 to the present*. Academic Century Press.

Wright, P. Elam, P. (2017). *Red Pill Psychology: Psychology For Men in a Gynocentric World*. Academic Century Press.

Wright, Peter. (October 2016), *Gynosympathy*. www.gynocentrism.com

Wollock, J. G. (2011). *Rethinking chivalry and courtly love*. (p. 42). ABC-CLIO.

Yalom, M., & Williams, C. (2012). *How the French Invented Love: Nine Hundred Years of Passion and Romance*. Harper Perennial.

3. What Ever Happened To Chivalry?

I have a Google alert for the word chivalry, and not a day goes by that I don't receive several articles on the topic. The articles appear slightly tilted toward the theme 'Male chivalry is dead,' followed by a reasonable number demonstrating 'Chivalry is alive and well' – the latter because some man, somewhere, risked life, limb or money to serve a woman's immediate welfare.

To be sure, chivalry displayed by individual men is on the decline, and women, men, government and mainstream media denounce this devolution with one voice: Men are becoming selfish pigs. MRAs and MGTOW choose to summarize it differently; that men are sick of being exploited and have chosen to shed their unnecessary selflessness.

Chivalry is documented in etiquette manuals of prior centuries explaining how a man is to take off his hat in a woman's presence, shake her hand, open doors, buy her gifts, and assist her in a multitude of ways. The message in these gestures is deference to the superiority of females:

> "If you see a lady whom you do not know, unattended, and wanting the assistance of a man, offer your services to her *immediately*. Do it with great courtesy, taking off your hat and begging the honour of assisting her." [Gynocentric etiquette for men – 1847]

> "In the familiar intercourse of society, a well-bred man will be known by the delicacy and deference with which he behaves towards females. That man would deservedly be looked upon as very deficient in proper respect and feeling, who should take any physical advantage of one of the weaker sex, or offer any personal slight towards her. Woman looks, and properly looks, for protection to man. It is the province

of the husband to shield the wife from injury; of the father to protect the daughter; the brother has the same duty to perform towards the sister; and, in general, every man should, in this sense, be the champion and the lover of every woman. Not only should he be ready to protect, but desirous to please, and willing to sacrifice much of his own personal ease and comfort, if, by doing so, he can increase those of any female in whose company he may find himself. Putting these principles into practice, a well-bred man, in his own house, will be kind and respectful in his behaviour to every female of the family. He will not use towards them harsh language, even if called upon to express dissatisfaction with their conduct. In conversation, he will abstain from every allusion which would put modesty to the blush. He will, as much as in his power, lighten their labors by cheerful and voluntary assistance. He will yield to them every little advantage which may occur in the regular routine of domestic life:—the most comfortable seat, if there be a difference; the warmest position by the winter's fireside; the nicest slice from the family joint, and so on." [Gynocentric etiquette for men – 1873]

"It must always be borne in mind that the assumption of Woman's social superiority lies at the root of these rules of conduct." [Gynocentric etiquette for men – 1897]

One reason for a decline of male chivalry is the vanishing payoff. Women no longer reciprocate for chivalry via good ol fashioned gestures like cooking, homemaking, praise, and affection that would have occurred at the time the above comments were penned. Today they don't even receive a thank you… is it any wonder men are seeing chivalry as a bad deal? The meal ticket, the flowers, the slaving at a job, the deference is all better spent on oneself.

Despite the hand-wringing over a decline in chivalry, women appear to be doing very well for themselves; they are well decked out with material goods, they display increasing body-freedom and body-pride, and their entry into workplace and careers is unprecedented. Society continues to indulge them as much as it ever did – *more*.

With this bare fact one might ask if chivalry merely *appears* to be on the decline and if women are receiving it from another source? My observation – obvious to many in the manosphere – is that they have corralled a rich new source of chivalry.

From Husband Sam to Uncle Sam

The heading is from Dr, Warren Farrell's *Myth of Male Power*, where he describes how men have traditionally striven to institute women-centered government by acting as women's proxy agents in the political sphere. This behavior, explains Farrell, is based on the chivalrous tradition of male servicing of women's needs. The following passage from Farrell's book explains the phenomenon:

> "Doesn't the fact that almost all legislators are men prove that men are in charge and can choose when to and when not to look out for women's interests? Theoretically, yes. But practically speaking the American legal system cannot be separated from the voter. And in the 1992 Presidential election , 54 percent of the voters were female, 46 percent were male. (Women's votes outnumber men's by more than 7 million). Overall, a legislator is to a voter what a chauffeur is to the employer – both look like they're in charge but both can be fired if they don't go where they're told. When legislators do not appear to be protecting women, it is almost always because women differ on what constitutes protection. (For example, women voted almost equally for Republicans and Democrats during the combination of the four presidential elections prior to Clinton).

> "The Government as Substitute Husband did for women what labor unions still have not accomplished for men. And men pay dues for labor unions; the taxpayer pays the dues for feminism. Feminism and government soon become taxpayer-supported women's unions. The political parties have become like two parents in a custody battle, each vying for their daughter's love by promising to do the most for her. How destructive to women is this? We have restricted humans from giving "free" food to bears and dolphins because we know that such feeding would make them

dependent and lead to their extinction. But when it comes to our own species, we have difficulty seeing the connection between short-term kindness and long-term cruelty: we give women money to have more children, making them more dependent with each child and discouraging them from developing the tools to fend for themselves. The real discrimination against women, then, is "free feeding."

Ironically, when political parties or parents compete for females' love by competing to give it, the result is not gratitude but entitlement. And the result should not be gratitude, because the political party, like the needy parent, becomes unconsciously dependent on keeping the female dependent. Which turns the female into "the other" — the person given to, not the equal participant. In the process, it fails to do what is every parent's and every political party's job — to raise an adult, not maintain a child.

But here's the rub. When the entitled child has the majority of the votes, the issue is no longer whether we have a patriarchy or a matriarchy — we get a victimarchy. And the female-as-child genuinely feels like a victim because she never learns how to obtain for herself everything she learns to expect. Well, she learns how to obtain it for herself by saying "it's a woman's right" — but she doesn't feel the mastery that comes with a lifetime of doing it for herself. And even when a quota includes her in the decision-making process, she still feels angry at the "male dominated government" because she feels both the condescension of being given "equality" and the contradiction of being given equality. She is still "the other." So, with the majority of the votes, she is both controlling the system and angry at the system." [The Myth of Male Power]

Do we need further evidence of "what ever happened to chivalry?" Not only have politicians taken over the job of chivalric appeasement of the ladies, it appears both the Left and Right of politics are jousting each other for the privilege to serve them. This I can understand… how else might they get elected?

John Stuart Mill, champion of feminism, urged shifting of the responsibility for chivalry out of the hands of every man and into the legislative framework of government proper, contending that chivalry was not always reliable and must give way to a more reliable, State-enforced protection and benevolence toward women. He writes:

> "From the combination of the two kinds of moral influence thus exercised by women, arose the spirit of chivalry: the peculiarity of which is to aim at combining the highest standard of the warlike qualities with the cultivation of a totally different class of virtues – those of gentleness, generosity, and self-abnegation towards the non-military and defenseless classes generally, and a special submission and worship directed towards women; who were distinguished from the other defenceless classes by the high rewards which they had it in their power voluntarily to bestow on those who endeavoured to earn their favour, instead of extorting their subjection…
>
> The main foundations of the moral life of modern times must be justice and prudence; the respect of each for the rights of every other, and the ability of each to take care of himself. Chivalry left without legal check all those forms of wrong

which reigned unpunished throughout society; it only encouraged a few to do right in preference to wrong, by the direction it gave to the instruments of praise and admiration. But the real dependence of morality must always be upon its penal sanctions – its power to deter from evil. The security of society cannot rest on merely rendering honour to right, a motive so comparatively weak in all but a few, and which on very many does not operate at all." [J. S. Mill: The Subjection of Women – 1869]

Ernest B. Bax confirms that the chivalric behavior of both Left and Right of politics was indeed, per Mill's suggestion, well underway by the year 1907:

"All parties, all sorts and conditions of politicians, from the fashionable and Conservative west-end philanthropist to the Radical working-men's clubbite, seem (or seemed until lately) to have come to an unanimous conclusion on one point – to wit, that the female sex is grievously groaning under the weight of male oppression." [Essays: New & Old (1907), pp.108-119]

Feminism draws its strength from chivalry, but instead of soliciting chivalry from men in the traditional, interpersonal manner it has learned how to get it in greater measure from the government – holding the government to ransom thanks to suffragettes gaining the vote for ~~gynocentrism~~ women.

Instead of men giving up seats in buses, government now provides seats in legislative assemblies and boardrooms via quotas. Instead of men opening car doors for women, government opens doors into universities and workforces via affirmative action. Instead of men being the sole protectors of women from violence, government now protects them with an army of police specially trained to service women's accusations (over and above more serious crimes). Instead of men providing living expenses, governments now provide it as social welfare and compensation for the 'wage gap'. Etc. …..
government as substitute husband.

All this compliments of feminism's pressuring the Left and Right into chivalric leadership. The only difference between the two sides of politics is that the Left is more sycophantic in its deliverance of chivalric rule – and the Right more heroic in its deliverance of chivalry. Same gynocentrism, different knight.

Left: St. George slays dragon   Right: George Bush pledges to rescue women from slavery

Left: Troubador supplicates a female audience with sweet songs   Right: President Obama

Gynocentric chivalry was an unbalanced idea to begin with. Men are slowly backing away from the custom, and we can yearn for the day government on both sides on the political fence does the same. Perhaps when the world's growing army of *grass eaters* brings about a collapse in revenue they will see the light. In the meantime, let's not give feminists a pass on their claim to have walked away from chivalry…. they have merely found a new source.

4. Sporting Tournaments: 'It Will Make A Man Out Of You'

A recent article by Doug Mortimer tells a story of a young man who went to a small town high school in the Texas Panhandle:

An avid tennis player, he went to the powers that be at his school and asked if he could form a tennis club. Sure, go ahead. Why not?

At first, things went well. Membership in the tennis club grew steadily. Then things went too well. Football players were dropping out in favor of the tennis club. So the powers that be changed their minds, and the tennis club was deep-sixed.

It is a curious paradox. In academic environments, where toxic masculinity is routinely excoriated, why is football, the ultimate contact sport – and arguably the most "toxic" sport – sacrosanct?

Musing on the story Mortimer goes on to conclude that what makes football different from other team sports, in least in terms of popular culture, is the belief that "it will make a man out of you":

In days of old, one could come right out and say that; today it's sub rosa. Other team sports, such as soccer, basketball, or baseball, are OK, but no one asserts they will make a man out of you. After all, even girls play soccer, basketball, and baseball (well, softball). But girls don't play football!

Athletic competition goes back at least as far as the ancient Greeks, but organized sports leagues are a relatively new phenomenon in civilization. The sociobiological take on them is they provide an arena for a ritualized form of aggression. Think of tribal warfare without spears.

So how did boys become men before football was invented? Playing games was a leisure activity at best. You could go your entire life without ever playing any kind of sport and no one would question your manhood.

This story and Mortimer's comments illustrate a fundamental contradiction at the heart of contemporary male-shaming, ie. the very things society shames men and boys for – in this case bone jarring football – are the very things that same society encourages. The double message for men and boys is never really resolved and they carry it like a lead weight.

Mortimer makes an important point here, and men in classical times didn't behave in the same way. Which begs the question of where, when and especially why did this ritualized form of competition come about? Historian Johan Huizinga provides an interesting answer to these questions:

"The warlike sports of the Middle Ages differ from Greek athletics by being far less simple and natural. Pride, honour, love and art give additional stimulus to the competition itself. Overloaded with pomp and decoration, full of heroic fancy, they serve to express romantic needs too strong for mere literature to satisfy. The realities of court life or a military career offered too little opportunity for the fine make-belief of heroism and love, which filled the soul. So they had to be acted. The staging of the tournament, therefore, had to be that of romance ; that is to say, the imaginary world of Arthur,

where the fancy of a fairy-tale was enhanced by the
sentimentality of courtly love."
[https://gynocentrism.com/2014/12/10/the-dream-of-
heroism-and-love-by-johan-huizinga/]

Based on Huizinga's account it seems the modern sporting
tournament was born first in France and referred to the joust, sword
fighting and other chivalric games, all of which seem to have their
origin in impressing women (who sat attentively in the stadiums) and
for the gaining of women's romantic attentions. Same thing today –
beautiful women lining up to fraternise with sports heroes, and
sportsmen and clubs doing special deeds for the ladies, from wearing
pink jerseys to raise money for breast cancer or raising awareness
about domestic violence, and generally engaging in gynocentric
deeds and gynosympathy.

And of course we have career feminists assisting sporting clubs in
the drafting of 'respecting women' charters that result in a more
general feminist oversight of club culture.

To underline the parallel I will finish this article with a series of
quotes that allow us to compare today's woman-impressing sports
culture with those of the Middle Ages, starting with a comment by
Thomas Warton in 1774:

> 'Many knights, says our Armoric fabler, famous for feats of
> chivalry, were present, with apparel and arms of the same
> colour and fashion. They formed a species of diversion, in
> imitation of a fight on horseback, and the ladies being placed
> on the walls of the castles, darted amorous glances on the
> combatants. None of these ladies esteemed any knight
> worthy of her love unless he had given proof of his gallantry
> in three fevered encounters. Thus the valour of the men
> encouraged chastity in the women, and the attention of the
> women proved an incentive to the soldier's bravery'
> [https://gynocentrism.com/2013/09/14/chivalry-for-love-
> 1774/]

The following is from Sir Walter Scott in 1818:

The looks, the words, the sign of a lady, were accounted to-
make knights at time of need perform double their usual
deeds of strength and valour. At tournaments and in combats,
the voices of the ladies were heard like those of the German
females in former battles, calling on the knights to remember
their fame, and exert themselves to the uttermost. "Think,
gentle knights," was their cry, "upon the wool of your
breasts, the nerve of your arms, the love you cherish in your
hearts, and do valiantly for ladies behold you." The
corresponding shouts of the combatants were, "Love of
ladies! Death of warriors! On, valiant knights, for you fight
under fair eyes? Where the honour or love of a lady was at
stake, the fairest prize was held out to the victorious knight,
and champion from every quarter were sure to hasten to
combat in a cause so popular.
[https://gynocentrism.com/2013/09/17/the-spirit-of-chivalry-
1818/]

The sporting tournament (from the French *tourney*) arose at
precisely the same time as romantic chivalry and courtly love, a
theme that continues today in the ubiquitous sporting tournament
everywhere. With this in mind it becomes the task of today's sports-
minded men to reflect on what and whom they are playing the game
for; for upper class women like those of medieval France, or for
simple, natural fun like the Greeks - or some other reason?

Figure 1: Female audience overseeing a medieval tournament

The following by Charles Mills (1825) documents further interaction between men and women at the first sports tournaments:

> The ladies were the supreme judges of tournaments, and if any complaint was raised against a knight, they adjudged the cause without appeal. Generally, however, they deputed their power to a knight, who, on account of this distinction, was called the *Knight of Honour*. He bore at the end of his lance a ribbon or some other sign of woman's favour, and with this badge of power he waved the fiercest knights into order and obedience.
>
> The heralds read to the knights the regulations of the sport, and announced the nature of the prize they were to contend for. The dames and maidens sometimes proposed jewels of price, a diamond, a ruby, and a sapphire, as rewards of valour. But the meed of renown was often more military, and the reader of Italian history remembers that at a tournament celebrated at Florence in the year 1468, Lorenzo de' Medici bore away the prize of a helmet of silver with a figure of Mars as the crest. It was the general wont of tournaments for a vanquished knight to forfeit his armour and horse to his victor.

Knights were led by ladies

> The knights then trooped to the listed a plain, with lords, ladies, and damsels, the chivalry and beauty of the country, mounted on gaily-caparisoned steeds and palfreys, whose housings swept the ground. Sometimes a lady fair led the horse of her chosen knight, and in the song of the minstrel the bridle became a golden chain of love. At the day appointed for a merry tournament, in the reign of Richard II., there issued out of the Tower of London, first, three-score coursers, apparelled for the lists, and on every one a squire of honour riding a soft pace.
>
> Then appeared three-score ladies of honour; mounted on fair palfreys, each lady leading by a chain of silver a knight sheathed in jousting harness. The fair and gallant troop, with

the sound of clarions, trumpets, and other minstrelsy, rode along the streets of London, the fronts of the houses shining with martial glory in the rich banners and tapestries which hung from the windows. They reached Smithfield where the Queen of England and many matrons and damsels were already seated in richly adorned galleries. The ladies that led the knights joined them; the squires of honour alighted from their coursers, and the knights in good order vaulted upon them.

Knights wore ladies' favours, who imitated the dress of knights

The tilting armour in which knights were sheathed was generally of a light fabric, and splendid. Its ornaments came under a gentler authority than that of royal constables and marshals. If the iron front of a line of cavaliers in the battle-field was frequently- gemmed with the variously coloured signs of ladies' favors, those graceful additions to armour yet more beseemed the tournament. Damsels were wont to surmount the helmets of their knights with chaplets, or to affix streamers to their spears, and a cavalier who was thus honoured smiled with self-complacency on the highly emblazoned surcoat of his rival in chivalry.

The desire to please ladies fair formed the very soul of the tournament. Every young and gallant knight wore the device of his mistress, while, indeed, the hardier sons of chivalry carried fiercer signs of their own achievements but they were unmarked by the bright judges of the tourney, for their eyes could only follow through the press their own emblems of love. Nothing was now to be heard but the noise and clattering of horse and armour.

Knights thanked by ladies

Every preux cavalier had by his side a lady bright. The minstrels tuned their harps to the praise of courtesy and prowess, and when the merriment was most joyous, the heralds presented to the ladies the knights who had worthily demeaned themselves. She, who by the consent at her fail companions was called *La Royne de la Beaulte et des Amours*, delivered the prizes to the kneeling knights. This queen of beauty and love addressed each of them with a speech of courtesy, thanking him for the disport and labour which he had taken that day, presenting to him the prize as the ladies' award for his skill, and concluding with the wish that such a valorous cavalier would have much joy and worship with his lady.

"The victory was entirely owing to the favor of my mistress, which I wore in my helmet," was the gallant reply of the knight, for he was always solicitous to exalt the honor of his lady-love. As tournaments were scenes of pleasure, the knight who appeared in the most handsome guise was praised and, to complete the courtesies of chivalry, thanks were rendered to those who had travelled to the lists from far countries.

Source: Charles Mills, *The History of Chivalry Or Knighthood and Its Times (1825)*

5. Intervening For Women

The "Enterprise of the Green Shield with the White Lady" (*Emprise de l'Escu vert à la Dame Blanche*) was a chivalric order founded by Jean Le Maingre and twelve knights in the year 1399, committing themselves to protecting women for a duration of five years. Inspired by the ideal of courtly love, the stated purpose of the order was to guard and defend the honor, estate, goods, reputation, fame and praise of all ladies, including widows. It was an undertaking that earned the praise of protofeminist Christine de Pizan.

Foundation

According to his *Livre des faits*, in 1399 Jean Le Maingre, tired of receiving complaints from ladies, maidens, and widows oppressed by powerful men bent on depriving them of the lands and honours, and finding no knight of squire willing to defend their just cause, decided out of compassion and charity to found an order of twelve knights sworn to carry "a shield of gold enamelled with green and a white lady inside" (*une targe d'or esmaillé de verd & tout une dame blanche dedans*). The twelve knights, after swearing this oath, affirmed a long letter explaining the purpose of their mission and disseminated it widely in France and beyond her borders.

The letter explained that any lady, young or old, finding herself the victim of injustices could petition one or more or the knights of the 'Enterprise of the Green Shield with the White Lady' for redress and that knight would respond promptly and leave whatever other task he was performing to fight the lady's oppressor personally. The twelve knights promised not just this, however. They offered also to release any other knight from a vow requiring him to fight a duel before a judge. The letter was signed 11 April 1399 by Jean le Maingre, Charles d'Albret, Geffroi le Maingre, François d'Aubrecicourt, Jean de Lignères, Chambrillac, Castelbayac, Gaucourt, Chasteaumorant, Betas, Bonnebaut, Colleville, and Torsay.

Symbols

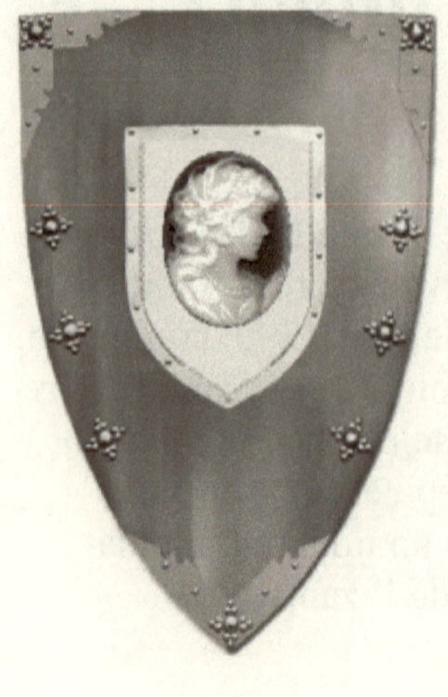

The emblem of the order was the shield of gold enamelled with green and a white lady inside. It seems reasonable to believe that the Dame Blanche represented the purity of women which the knights of the order were to protect. What the green background signified is not clear, but it is known that white and green were sometimes associated together in connection with the observances of May, as is shown by an account in Hall's *Chronicle* of a "maying" of Henry VIII of England, in which the company were clad in green on one occasion and in white on another. In Machyn's *Diary*, too, there is mention of a white and green Maypole around which danced a company of men and women wearing "baldrykes" of white and green.

More important to the theme of chivalry is that *The Order of the Green Shield with the White Lady* bears a striking resemblance to the so-called "White Ribbon Campaigns" of today that require men, as was required of the medieval knights above, to pledge oaths to "Never to condone, or remain silent about violence towards women and girls" and especially *to intervene* when learning of any male behaving badly toward a female. The continuity of chivalry in these two examples is striking, revealing a seamless perpetuation of the convention to the present day.

Sources:

Lalande, Denis (1988). Jean II Le Meingre, dit Boucicaut (1366–1421): étude d'une biographie héroïque.
Marsh, George L. (1906) "Sources and Analogues of 'The Flower and the Leaf': Part I." Modern Philology, pp. 153.
Riquer, Martín de (1967). Caballeros andantes españoles. Madrid: Editorial Espasa-Calpe.

6. Chivalry: A Learned Deathwish

Just after midnight last Friday, April 22, 2016, and a scant 4 or 5 miles from where I am sitting, 19-year-old Jason Cisneros stopped by his best friend Ivania's apartment to see her. When he arrived, he heard a commotion near where he parked.

He sent a text to Ivania inside, saying, "'I'm outside. There's a lady honking, and this guy wants to hit her. He wants to kill her."

Jason then approached the woman's car to intervene. Just a moment later, he lay dying on the street, with two gunshot wounds.

The news coverage on this, what little it will get, will paint a simple picture. A brave young man heard a woman in distress — a woman he did not even know — and lost his life trying to protect her.

Of course, the real story is not nearly so simple. What made this young man walk into the line of fire? Was it heroics? Why didn't he just call the police? Why did he feel the pull toward intervening in the troubles of a female stranger?

Why have men like this, rushing in and dying to protect women they don't even know, become their own crime statistic?

This is a sad event that illustrates so much of what is wrong with men's story in the modern age.

With the narrative about men's place in the world casting them in the role of a protective vassal, we have developed the expectation that this is what men ought to be.

Undoubtedly the news coverage will play this out as a senseless tragedy. Accordingly, most will eventually take refuge in the fanciful idea that Jason Cisneros died a hero.

The members of society, by and large, who read this story and watch the news video, will end up on a similar trajectory, toward glorifying the self-sacrifice.

They will not conclude that this was a young man who was set up, duped into putting his neck on the chopping block by a history and force he never had a chance to grow up to understand.

His parents will take solace in the idea that their son died doing something noble. His friend will apply a similar salve to her grief. Few, if any, will question the wisdom of his choice or the factors that drove him to make it.

Fewer still will wonder about the character of the woman he was trying to save, even though it was evident that she was in a relationship with a murderous thug, that her chickens had come home to roost that night, and that she wanted someone to rescue her at any cost.

Jason Cisneros died trying to protect a woman he did not know, who it turns out may have been no more worthy of protection than the man who killed him.

Our society will interpret his death as heroics, and thus teach more young men that this insanity is the model of manhood they should emulate.

We will deny our young men the truth. Jason's impulse to rescue the damsel in distress is a dysfunctional mandate passed down from generation to generation living by a narrative that sees his life as easily disposable.

Was Jason a good man? Most probably he was, though I am loathe to use that term lightly anymore. There is too much pointless sacrifice that comes with it.

The small amount of information that I have indicates that he came from a loving, supportive and close-knit family. And he was, after all, doing what he believed to be the right thing.

I can't even imagine the sense of loss his family feels right now. Parents burying a child instead of the reverse is a hugely painful deviation from the natural order.

But for the sake of preventing more funerals, it is important to push aside the misguided chivalry and false heroism of this event and recognize that Jason's death is one of countless, pointless sacrifices that never should have happened.

There is nothing to glorify here. Not the death of a beloved son. Not the ill-fated choices of young women who are sexually excited by criminality and violence.

And not the false code of male honor inflicted on young men from the shadows of a warped social consciousness.

There is a lesson here for parents and for anyone else who has a young man in their lives whom they love.

Please ask yourself, if your son or other loved one encountered the same situation as Jason, what would they do? Would they intervene? If they did, is that what you would want them to do?

Would it make you proud? If it would, are you willing to bury them for the sake of that pride?

If you would not want your son to die like Jason Cisneros died, have you told him? Have you made it clear to him that dying for a stranger is not your idea of manhood?

Have the lessons from your family been about protecting his loved ones, protecting himself, or about protecting anyone at his own expense?

You know, this stuff matters. Today's young men get copious amounts of messaging about manhood, most of it instructing them to accept their disposability by calling it a badge of honor.

Young men face a barrage of social messages to "man up" and be a "real man" and other shaming, exploitive instructions.

It even comes from the government. We see it in the "It's On Us" anti-sexual assault campaign, which includes President Obama and Vice-President Joe Biden, along with stars like Common, Mike Roe, and others, telling young men that it is on them to intervene.

Just like Jason Cisneros did.

Please watch the **"It's On Us" video** and think about the price Jason paid for making sure it was on him.

Doing that might make you stop to consider if you want to manipulate your son or another beloved man into playing unarmed and unpaid bodyguard, ever at the disposal of strangers.

And while you're at it, you might ask yourself something else. Do you have any reason to think Common would risk his life for a stranger?

Do you think Joe Biden, author of the Violence Against Women Act cares about your son — or the women's vote?

When I look at what Jason's story turned into, all I see is a devastated family, a grieving friend, and a decent young man with a life cut short on behalf of someone who in no way warranted that kind of sacrifice – not that any stranger ever does.

Perhaps there is a better social message we can send all people, young and old. It's on you.

It's on you to forge the ability to protect yourself. It's on you to make sound decisions about people with whom you choose to get involved.

It is not the responsibility of strangers, and it is not a burden for another class of human beings to bear.

No one outside you, your family and the police have any obligation to take risks for your safety. If women don't know this, the parents of young men certainly should.

7. Death by Chivalry: Portland Edition

Let's talk about what happened in Portland. The story that we know is simple; three men confronted a lunatic that was harassing a couple of women on the train, one of them a Muslim woman wearing a hijab. Minutes later two of them had been stabbed to death and one of them had been seriously wounded.

Predictably the stabbing victims were lauded across the world, and the word 'hero' was being tossed around like condoms in a cat house. Naturally being of red pill mentality and a men's advocate I'm wary of the word hero, mainly because it is so often written on epitaphs and because it is so frequently used to manage grief, a way for loved ones to figure out how to live with a senseless tragedy.

And it is not that I'd begrudge them that simple refuge. If believing that a dead son, brother or father gave his life in an act of heroism helps assuage a devastating loss, then I can't fault families for clinging to it. But on a wider social level just slapping a sticker that says hero on a coffin and spruiking mindlessly about gallantry is a little less functional.

A good bit less, actually.

After the incident in Portland Twitter lit up with activity about it, including this tweet:

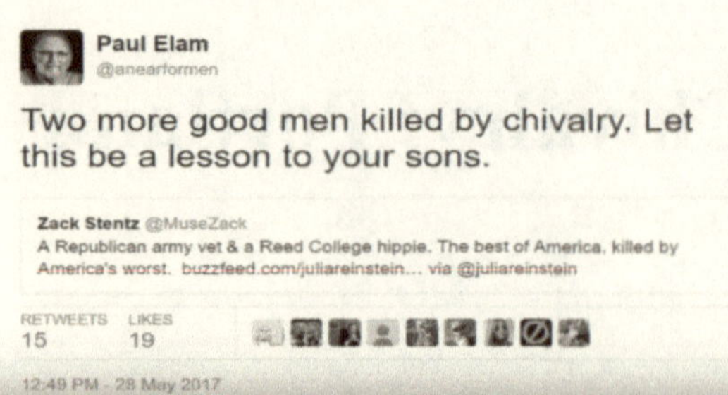

Two more good men killed by chivalry. Let this be a lesson to your sons. I tweeted that over 24 hours ago and the butthurt reactions to it are still rolling in.

The Real Men gynotrad brigade showed up early, and with gusto. They were accompanied by feminists trying to outdo the gynotrads on being righteously indignant about what I said.

There was even an MRA who chimed in, as some MRAs do, with instructions on what I should or should not say because you know, reasons.

So here I am, witnessing a virtual Slutwalk of traditional men, feminist women and a quasi-MRA bringing up the rear, all chiding me about being a coward, or worse a man who doesn't care about women.

With enough demands for male gallantry and sacrifice to make Christina Hoff-Sommers smile in approval, I've been treated to the full range of socially demanded expectations of men, and likewise women's immunity from said obligations.

Now it would be easy, even entertaining to wipe the spittle off the tweets and respond to them directly for this analysis, but I have a better idea.

Why don't we look at what happened on that train in Portland and see if I'm right, or if I'm wrong.

According to the news reports and witness statements, what happened seems clear. I do want to issue the caveat though that the word *seems* is important. I say that because recently I gave Aleksandr Kolpakov credit for the possibility that he suffered combat related PTSD after murdering his sceptic feminist co-host. Turns out he never deployed - he was a much more garden variety murderer.

Anyway, back to Portland. The news reports say that the madman whose name does not merit repeating, confronted two young women and started berating them with ethnic insults. The women reportedly retreated to the back of the train while at least one of the stabling victims confronted the madman, were arguing, and ultimately deadly violence occurred.

There is nothing in any of the reports I read, and I read several, that indicated the killer was in the pursuit of the two women to the back of the train. Nothing in fact that indicated there was any physical threat to those women at all.

To put a fine point on it, there was no violence till the so-called heroes intervened. And so let's talk about that intervention, because in my mind that's where the rubber meets the road.

One CNN report stated that the victims approached the killer and tried to calm him down. It appears that this however is not entirely true. One of the women, Destinee Mangum, gave the following account to CNN in another report: "Then a stranger intervened" she said, telling the man that "he can't disrespect these young ladies like that." Then they all just started arguing, she said.

Now, think about that for a moment. The man was clearly agitated and mentally unstable. His original targets, the women, wisely moved away and gave him a wide berth. One of the men however according to Mangum stepped in and told the killer "that he can't disrespect these young ladies like that." Then the violence happened.

Now I want to point out however briefly that she did not quote the man as saying that you can't assault these young ladies like that, that you can't threaten these young ladies like that, that you can't rape these young ladies like that. It was you can't *disrespect* these young ladies like that.

At this point one of the stabbing victims was reacting to two women being disrespected. For that he gave his life, and so did one other man. I say that because it's very important here to establish that these men didn't step up to protect anyone from anything but the hateful ranting of an asshole.

They died protecting two women from harsh words. And for that we have the entire Western world heaping praise on them. Posthumously, of course.

And there's another point here that can't be ignored. I've worked in many psychiatric facilities and in one correctional facility. In that work it was routinely expected that I was able to have a calming effect on agitated and often violence prone people. It was quite a challenge at times.

One thing I can tell you though, both from experience and fundamental common sense, if you want to calm an agitated person down you won't get the job done by moving into their space and telling them they just can't insult people. Matter of fact, I can pretty much assure you that the effect of this approach will pretty much define the opposite of calming.

Stepping up to an irrationally angry, verbally abusive stranger and telling them that they just can't insult the little ladies isn't the act of someone intent on diffusing a tense situation. It's the showboating of a white knight who probably doesn't have a real clue about what exactly is motivating him to act so mindlessly.

I know, this is where the decency police come in, in a Twitter rage I bet, aghast that I could come to such a conclusion. This is where the people on Twitter challenged my manhood, called me a coward and a few other choice names, and even asked me if my mother had ever loved me. All because I came to a conclusion based on the evidence instead of switching into hero-worship mode and encouraging all men to find honor in this kind of death.

Sorry, but I'm not buying it for a second.

Those two men had families, people who loved them. And being men they very likely had people counting on them, needing them, who will now never be able to count on them for anything again.

Because you just can't insult these young ladies.

Call me a coward if you want. Question my manhood, I don't care. I've been beyond caring about that sort of thing for a long time now. And besides, if you ask me, the hero-worshippers are the only real cowards in this picture.

If I've learned one thing about needless deaths like this it is that it brings the decency brigade right out of the shadows every time. They crow about the mindless heroics of dead boys, and urge more boys to emulate the fatally stupid antics of modern chivalry.

People like this are always putting young men who give their life for nothing on pedestals, right where they can admire them. As long as someone else is doing the dying. As long as they are providing a real life Rambo movie for someone else's vicarious enjoyment. Every time I see it happen I want nothing more than to change the channel. This movie always ends the same way. All I can hope for is that a few more people each time will see through the haze of hero worship and let that be a lesson for their sons.

Sources:

CNN Report #1: https://edition.cnn.com/2017/05/26/us/portland-train-stabbing/

CNN Report #2: https://edition.cnn.com/2017/05/29/us/portland-train-teenager-stabbing/

8. Aggrieved Entitlement: Women's Reaction to Temporary Loss Of Chivalry

It's no secret that women feel entitled to special treatments from men based on the European culture tradition of chivalry: i.e., allowing women to go through the door first; showering the "fairer sex" with compliments about being beautiful, caring or pure; paying for dinner and other life luxuries; and offering them costly care and protection around the clock. In the modern context chivalry boils down to the male posture of *deference to women's needs and wants*, which understandably fosters a positive self-concept in women and a sense that they must be "worth it" as we are reminded by the ubiquitous advertising jingle.

The expectation of male chivalry, or benevolent sexism as some prefer to call it, is nothing new and there are countless studies confirming that women generally expect such treatment from men.[1] So we will take that expectation as a given. What hasn't been studied sufficiently in women is the reaction men's *failure* to provide expected level of chivalric supplies, and this is where we run into the useful concept of 'aggrieved entitlement.'

The phrase aggrieved entitlement was popularized by feminist Michael Kimmel who refers to it as a gendered emotion displayed by disenfranchised males, entailing "a fusion of that humiliating loss of manhood and the moral obligation and entitlement to get it back."[2] By 'manhood' Kimmel is referring to rights that males have supposedly enjoyed over women and culture that are subsequently denied them by a changing world. He further clarifies that men "tend to feel their sense of aggrieved entitlement because of the past; they want to restore what they *once had*. Their entitlement is not aspirational; its nostalgic."[3]

In a recent paper Dennis Gouws suggests that the aggrieved entitlement descriptor can be equally applied to the behavior of women. Reviewing Kimmel's concept he concludes:

> Because Kimmel's sympathies lie with gender feminism, he is uninterested in how this concept might apply to women's behavior. Women might express aggrieved entitlement when they experience what they perceive to be a humiliating loss of the gynocentric privilege to which gynocentric chivalry, gender feminism, and hegemonic gynarchy have entitled them. Self-righteous, angry expressions of personal offense and even violent acts might result from their perceived moral obligation to regain their sense of gynocentric privilege. A cursory internet search of gender-feminist responses to men's-issues speakers on campus and to the establishing men's groups or other male-positive spaces on campus will provide examples of this aggrieved entitlement.[4]

Gouws provides a useful example of aggrieved entitlement by women who dominate university campus culture. Men attempting to establish male support groups on female-dominated campuses, or who attempt to invite speakers sympathetic to men's health issues, have frequently been met with fury for apparently removing the chivalric focus from women and their issues. The resultant female rage has triggered violent protests, intimidation, vindictive and false accusations, or boycotting of male initiatives through financial and other means.

Looking at the sexual-relations contract that has been operating for eons we can see that a certain degree of narcissistic pride was encouraged in order to sweeten gender roles for men and women – "He's an awesome strong man, a man's man and a great provider" or "She's a magnificent mother, those children never go without love or food". Those adhering to traditional gender roles received compliments for their service, along with some compensatory payoffs by the opposite sex.

When an individual fails to adhere to their traditional gender role the bubble of narcissistic pride bursts, giving rise to aggrieved entitlement in members of the opposite sex. In the language of psychology we would say the expectation of narcissistic supply has been cut off, and narcissistic injury and rage steps forward to address the grievance. Most readers would know that some of the worst examples of aggrieved entitlement by women are displayed by feminists, about whose behavior Ernest B. Bax was able to conclude, "Weakness, to whose claim chivalry may per se be granted, forfeits its claim when it *presumes* upon that claim and becomes aggressive. Aggressive weakness deserves no quarter."[5]

Bax further elaborates on aggressive weakness (i.e., aggrieved entitlement) in the following passages:

> I may point out in conclusion that the existing state of public opinion on the subject registers the fact that sex-conscious women have exploited the muscular weakness of their sex and have succeeded in forging a weapon of tyranny called "chivalry" which enables them to ride rough-shod over every principle of justice and fair play. Men are cowed by it, and fail to distinguish between simple weakness per se which should command every consideration, and that of *aggressive* weakness which trades upon "chivalry" and deserves no quarter.[6]

> "Even taking the matter on the conventional ground of weakness and granting, for the sake of argument, the relative muscular weakness of the female as ground for her being allowed the immunity claimed by Modern Feminists of the sentimental school, the distinction is altogether lost sight of between weakness as such and *aggressive weakness*. Now I submit there is a very considerable difference between what is due to weakness that is harmless and unprovocative, and weakness that is *aggressive*, still more when this *aggressive* weakness presumes on itself as weakness, and on the consideration extended to it, in order to become tyrannical and oppressive. Weakness as such assuredly deserves all consideration, but *aggressive* weakness deserves none save to be crushed beneath the iron heel of strength. Woman at the present day has been encouraged by a Feminist public opinion to become meanly aggressive under the protection of her weakness. She has been encouraged to forge

her gift of weakness into a weapon of tyranny against man, unwitting that in so doing she has deprived her weakness of all just claim to consideration or even to toleration."[7]

Bax penned the above observations over a century ago, although the behavior he described had been around for much longer than that. The phrase 'Hell hath no fury like a woman scorned' is usually attributed to the English playwright and poet William Congreve. He wrote these lines in his play The Mourning Bride, 1697:

> Heav'n has no Rage, like Love to Hatred turn'd,
> Nor Hell a Fury, like a Woman scorn'd.

These lines describe a temporary loss of male chivalry by women and the aggrieved entitlement that ensues – a reaction that Michael Kimmel pretentiously emphasizes as a mostly male pathology. A more honest appraisal of the changing gender roles and the accompanying sense of aggrieved entitlement would admit that women's roles and choices have expanded exponentially, which includes the throwing off of *any* expected responsibilities toward men and boys, while conversely the male role of providing benevolent sexism/chivalry for women has changed little. On the basis of such disparity men appear to be coping remarkably well in comparison to women who retain many of their traditional privileges and expectations, but who display extreme rage at micro-disenfranchisements and momentary lapses in chivalric supply.

In summary the grief-reaction over loss of traditional roles is not a predominately male issue. Women have yet to experience the loss of gendered entitlements on anywhere near the same scale as men, however they are equally proficient at raging over micro-losses of chivalry and male deference. The theory of aggrieved entitlement thus applies to no gender in particular – so lets use it to describe the ever-present rage displayed by women in both private and public settings.

References:

[1] Hammond, M. D., Sibley, C. G., & Overall, N. C. *The allure of sexism: Psychological entitlement fosters women's endorsement of*

benevolent sexism over time. Social Psychological and Personality Science, 5(4), 422-429. (2014)
[2] Kalish, R., & Kimmel, M. *Suicide by mass murder: Masculinity, aggrieved entitlement, and rampage school shootings.* Health Sociology Review, 9(4), 451–464. (2010)
[3] Kimmel, Michael. *Angry white men: American masculinity at the end of an era.* Hachette UK, (2017).
[4] Dennis Gouws, *Not So Romantic For Men: Using Sir Walter Scott's Ivanhoe to Explore Evolving Notions of Chivalry*, in Voicing the Silences of Social and Cognitive Justice, 167–178. (2018)
[5] Ernest B. Bax., *Women's Privileges and "Rights", Social Democrat*, Vol.13 no.9, September (1909).
[6] Ernest B. Bax., *Feminism and Female Suffrage* in New Age, (1910)
[7] Ernest B. Bax., Chapter 5: The "Chivalry" Fake, in *The Fraud of Feminism* (1913)

9. Can a woman be chivalrous?

Chivalry is today seen as a mostly male obligation toward female beneficiaries. In the past there were exceptions showing that "chivalry" could be applied equally to women who demonstrated it.

Stripped of the usual gender conventions, romantic chivalry is nothing more than displays of altruism and generosity toward another human being. The sooner women start extending such "chivalry" toward men and boys, and calling it "chivalry," the sooner we might call relationships reciprocal. Until then we will continue to see male-only chivalry by actors on a gynocentric stage.

A few examples of 'female chivalry' discovered in earlier literature follow with dates:

Female chivalry

> 1792 "Mr. Burke remarked, that however the spirit of chivalry may be in the decline amongst men, the age of *female chivalry* was just commencing."

> 1918 "Spenser, following Ariosto, laments the decay of *female chivalry* since the days of Penthesilia, Deborah, and Camilla."

> 1938 "This tendency among women of making concessions to men for their inferior moral strength I would like to term "*female chivalry*." It is chivalry in the strictest sense of the term because it makes concessions for the weakness of the opposite side. In a society which is so primitive that its women have not yet developed in their conduct with men this moral chivalry, no doubt the woman is an inferior and subordinate member, an object of masculine pity. But the moment she brings into play upon the field of our social behaviour her superior moral strength (manifested through the developments of her inherent powers of sacrifice, endurance and self-discipline) she not only qualifies herself

for equality of treatment but records a moral victory of first magnitude over the opposite sex."

Woman's chivalry

1847 "It may be, too, that such pursuits belong to *woman's chivalry*, in which she accomplishes tender victories, and with silken cords leads into bondage the stouter heart of man. Happy triumph: in which there is equal delight to the victor and the vanquished."

1924 "There are poems of the human soul cut off from God by its lovelessness — the hell of separation of the finite self from the infinite; poems of the "white flame" of a greater love; *woman's chivalry* towards woman ; *woman's chivalry* towards man: and in the end, peace."

1936 "Neuilly, but something — perhaps a *woman's chivalry* to another woman — prevented her from doing it."

Chivalric female

1864 "The order of Sisters of Charity, therefore, as constituted by St. Vincent de Paul, and whose deeds are known to the whole world, may be considered an aristocratic or *chivalric female* army of volunteers of charity, bound to short terms of service, but generally renewing their vows, and performing prodigies of usefulness."

Chivalrous women

1857 "It must be confessed that the spectacle of those three *chivalrous women*, so magnanimous in face of an evil cause… preparing to plunge into the medley of battle, instead of remaining at a distance to watch the fortune of the fray, instead too of shutting themselves up in some luxurious dwelling there to await the intelligence of the result – but armed and mounted – with martial plumes waving over their heads, fire in their eyes and decision on their lips… could have no other effect than the most inspiring one over those who beheld it."

1896 "For a lady is among other things a woman with a sense of chivalry, and a *chivalrous woman* uses her finer gifts to supplement the blunt honesty of her husband (if she is the happy possessor of an honest husband)."

1904 "The self-sacrificing *chivalrous woman,* with whom duty is a first consideration."

1906 "Those *chivalrous Women* seem to be chosen instruments for the world's betterment—all in the general economy of nature — evidence of growth which sometimes takes us by surprise and makes us sit up and think."

1912 "Yes — women can he chivalrous! — women can live and die for a conviction! My terrible confession is made easier by your belief!"

1918 "to the free and *chivalrous women* of America."

1919 "they called upon the free and *chivalrous women* of America to make these wrongs their own and, in so far as possible, to try to redress them, and to safeguard the future of the race by standing for the independence of historic Armenia."

1920 "This mighty work of hospital redemption, now so nearly accomplished in all civilized countries, so appealed to *chivalrous women* that there seemed no end to the stream of incoming probationers."

Chivalric woman

1897 "We are glad to know that such a noble and *chivalric woman* has her being among the toilers of the overwrought East End, and trust that her good deeds have not gone unrewarded."

We live in a time now of great convenience, and if relationships are to mean anything going forward they will need to be based on some kind of reciprocal chivalry. And the good news is that men and women can demonstrate their brands of chivalry differently if they wish - a 'co-chivalry' that can be respectful of similarities or differences as agreed between individual men and women.

SELECTION OF HISTORICAL SOURCES

Chivalry For Love (1774)

"At the ideal coronation of king Arthur, just mentioned, a tournament is described as exhibited in its highest splendor.

> 'Many knights, says our Armoric fabler, famous for feats of chivalry, were present, with apparel and arms of the same colour and fashion. They formed a species of diversion, in imitation of a fight on horseback, and the ladies being placed on the walls of the castles, darted amorous glances on the combatants. None of these ladies esteemed any knight worthy of her love unless he had given proof of his gallantry in three fevered encounters. Thus the valour of the men encouraged chastity in the women, and the attention of the women proved an incentive to the soldier's bravery'

Here is the practice of chivalry under the combined ideas of love and military prowess, as they seem to have subsisted after the feudal constitution had acquired greater degrees not only of stability but of splendor and refinement.

***

"And hence, even in time of peace, they had no conception of any diversions or public ceremonies, except of the military kind. Yet, as the courts of these petty princes were thronged with ladies of the most eminent distinction and quality, the ruling passion for war was tempered with courtesy.

The prize of contending champions was adjudged by the ladies; who did not think it inconsistent to be present or to preside at the bloody spectacles of the times ; and who, themselves, seem to have contracted an unnatural and unbecoming ferocity, while they softened the manners of those valorous knights who fought for their approbation.

The high notions of a noble descent, which arose from the condition of the feudal constitution, and the ambition of forming an alliance with powerful and opulent families, cherished this romantic system. It was hard to obtain the fair feudatary, who was the object of universal adoration. Not only the splendor of birth, but the magnificent castle surrounded with embattled walls, guarded with massive towers, and crowned with lofty pinnacles, served to inflame the imagination, and to create an attachment to some illustrious heiress, whose point of honour it was to be chaste and inaccessible.

And the difficulty of success on these occasions, seems in great measure to have given rife to that sentimental love of romance, which acquiesced in a distant respectful admiration, and did not aspire to possession… Chivalry by degrees was consecrated by religion, whose authority tinctured every passion, and was engrafted into every institution, of the superstitious ages ; and at length composed that familiar picture of manners, in which the love of a god and of the ladies were reconciled, the saint and the hero were blended, and charity and revenge, zeal and gallantry, devotion and valour, were united.

***

"But the principal subject of the poems, dictated in great measure by the spirit of chivalry, was love: especially among the troubadours of rank and distinction, whose castles being crowded with ladies, presented perpetual scenes of the most splendid gallantry. This passion they spiritualifed into various metaphysical refinements, and filled it with abstracted notions of visionary perfection and felicity.

Source: Chapter one of 'On The Origin of Romantic Fiction in Europe' (1774)

The Spirit Of Chivalry (1818)

The main ingredient in the spirit of Chivalry, second in force only to the religious zeal of its professors, and frequently predominating over it, was a devotion to the female sex, and particularly to her whom each knight selected as the chief object of his affection, of a nature so extravagant and unbounded as to approach to a sort of idolatry. The original source of this sentiment is to be found, like that of Chivalry itself, in the Customs and habits of the northern tribes who possessed, even in their rudest state, so many honourable and manly distinctions, over all the other nations in the same stage of society. The chaste and temperate habits of these youth, and the opinion that it was dishonourable to hold sexual intercourse until the twentieth year was attained, was in the highest degree favourable not only to the morals and health of the ancient Germans, but must have contributed greatly to place their females in that dignified and respectable rank which they held in society.

***

Amid the various duties of knighthood, that of protecting the female sex, respecting their persons, and redressing their wrongs, becoming the champion of their cause, and the chastiser of those by whom they were injured, was represented as one of the principal objects of the institution. Their oath bound the new-made knights to defend the cause of all women without exception ; and the most pressing way of conjuring them to grant a boon was to implore it in the name of God and the ladies. The cause of a distressed lady was, in many instances, preferable to that even of the country to which the knight belonged. Thus, the Captal de Buche, though an English subject, did not hesitate to unite his troops with those of the Comte de Foix, to relieve the ladies in a French town, where they were besieged and threatened with violence by the insurgent peasantry.

The looks, the words, the sign of a lady, were accounted to- make knights at time of need perform double their usual deeds of strength and valour. At tournaments and in combats, the voices of the ladies were heard like those of the German females in former battles, calling on the knights to remember their fame, and exert themselves to the uttermost. "Think, gentle knights," was their cry, "upon the wool of your breasts, the nerve of your arms, the love you cherish in your hearts, and do valiantly for ladies behold you." The corresponding shouts of the combatants were, "Love of ladies! Death of warriors! On, valiant knights, for you fight under fair eyes? Where the honour or love of a lady was at stake, the fairest prize was held out to the victorious knight, and champion from every quarter were sure to hasten to combat in a cause so popular. Chaucer, when he describes the assembly of the knights who came with Arcite and Palemon to fight for the love of the fair Emilie, describes the manners of his age in the following lines;

> "For every knight that loved chivalry,
> And would his thankes have a passant name,
> Hath pray'd that he might ben of that game,
> And well was him that thereto chusen was.
> For if there fell to-morrow such a case,
> Ye knowen well that every lusty knight
> That loveth par amour, and hath his might,
> Were it in Engellande, or elleswhere,
> They wold hir thanked willen to be there.
> To fight for a lady! Ah! Benedicite,
> It were a lusty sight for to see."

It is needless to multiply quotations on a subject so trite and well known. The defence of the female sex in general, the regard due to their honour, the subservience paid to their commands, the reverent awe and courtesy, which, in their presence, forbear all unseemly words and actions, were so blended with the institution of Chivalry as to form its very essence. But it was not enough that the "very perfect, gentle knight," should reverence the fair sex in general. It was essential to his character that he should select, as his proper choice, "a lady and a love," to be the polar star of his thoughts, the mistress of his affections, and the directress of his actions. In her service, he was to observe the duties of loyalty, faith, secrecy, and reverence.

Without such an empress of his heart, a knight, in the phrase of the times, was a ship without a rudder, a horse without a bridle, a sword without a hilt ; a being, in short, devoid of that ruling guidance and intelligence, which ought to inspire his bravery, and direct his actions. The least dishonest thought or action was, according to her doctrine, sufficient to forfeit the chivalrous lover the favour of his lady. It seems, however, that the greater part of her charge concerning incontinence is levelled against such as haunted the receptacles of open vice ; and that she reserved an exception (of which, in the course of the history, she made liberal use) in favour of the intercourse which, in all love, honour, and secrecy, might take place, when the favoured and faithful knight had obtained, by long service, the boon of amorous mercy from the lady whom he loved par amours.

In these extracts are painted the actual manners of the age of Chivalry. The necessity of the perfect knight having a mistress, whom he loved par amours, the duty of dedicating his time to obey her commands, however capricious, and his strength to execute extravagant feats of valour, which might redound to her praise, –for all that was done for her sake, and under her auspices, was counted her merit, as the victories of their generals were ascribed to the Roman Emperors— was not a whit less necessary to complete the character of a good knight.

****

On such occasions, the favoured knight, as he wore the colours and badge of the lady of his affections, usually exerted his ingenuity in inventing some device or cognisance which might express their love, either openly, as boasting of it in the eye of the world, or in such mysterious mode of indication as should only be understood by the beloved person if circumstances did not permit an avowal of his passion. The ladies, bound as they were in honour to requite the passion of their knights, were wont, on such occasions, to dignify them by the present of a scarf, ribbon, or glove, which was to be worn in the press of battle and tournament. These marks of favour they displayed on their helmets, and they were accounted the best incentives to deeds of valour. The custom appears to have prevailed in France to a late period, though polluted with the grossness so often mixed with the affected refinement and gallantry of that nation.

Sometimes the ladies, in conferring these tokens of their favour, saddled the knights with the most extravagant and severe conditions. But the lover had his advantage in such cases, that if he ventured to encounter the hazard imposed, and chanced to survive it, he had, according to the fashion of the age, the right of exacting, from the lady, favours corresponding in importance. The annals of Chivalry abound with stories of cruel and cold fair ones, who subjected their lovers to extremes of danger, in hopes that they might get rid of their addresses, but were, upon their unexpected success, caught in their own snare, and, as ladies who would not have their name made the theme of reproach by every minstrel, were compelled to recompense the deeds which their champion had achieved in their name.

Lady's shift garment

There are instances in which the lover used his right of reprisals with some rigour, as in the well-known fabliau of the three knights and the shift; in which a lady proposes to her three lovers, successively, the task of entering, unarmed, into the mêlée of a tournament, arrayed only in one of her shift. The perilous proposal is declined by two of the knights and accepted by the third, who thrusts himself, in the unprotected state required, into all the hazards of the tournament, sustains many wounds, and carries off the prize of the day. On the next day the husband of the lady (for she was married) was to give a superb banquet to the knights and nobles who had attended the tourney. The wounded victor sends the shift back to its owner, with his request, that she would wear it over her rich dress on this solemn occasion, soiled and torn as it was, and stained all over with the blood of its late wearer. The lady did not hesitate to comply, declaring, that she regarded this shift, stained with the blood of her "fair friend, as more precious than if it were of the most costly materials." Jaques de Basin, the minstrel who relates this curious tale, is at a loss to say whether the palm of true love should be given to the knight or to the lady on this remarkable occasion. The husband, he assures us, had the good sense to seem to perceive nothing uncommon in the singular vestment with which his lady was attired, and the rest of the good company highly admired her courageous requital of the knight's gallantry.

It was the especial pride of each distinguished champion, to maintain, against all others, the superior worth, beauty, and accomplishments of his lady; to bear her picture from court to court, and support, with lance and sword, her superiority to all other dames, abroad or at home. To break a spear for the love of their ladies, was a challenge courteously given, and gently accepted, among all true followers of Chivalry, and history and romance are alike filled with the tilts and tournaments which took place upon this argument, which was ever ready and ever acceptable. Indeed, whatever the subject of the tournament had been, the lists were never closed until a solemn course had been made in honour of the ladies. There were knights yet more adventurous, who sought to distinguish themselves by singular and uncommon feats of arms in honour of their mistresses; and such was usually the cause of the whimsical and extravagant vows of arms which we have subsequently to notice. To combat against extravagant odds, to fight amid the press of armed knights without some essential part of their armour, to do some deed of audacious valour in face of friend and foe, were the services by which the knights strove to recommend themselves, or which their mistresses (very justly so called) imposed on them as proofs of their affection.

Sometimes the patience of the lover was worn out by the cold-hearted vanity which thrust him on such perilous enterprises. At the court of one of the German emperors, while some ladies and gallants of the court were looking into a den where two lions were confined, one of them purposely let her glove fall within the palisade which enclosed the animals, and commanded her lover, as a true knight, to fetch it out to her. He did not hesitate to obey, jumped over the enclosure ; threw his mantle towards the animals as they sprung at him; snatched up the glove, and regained the outside of the palisade. But when in safety, he proclaimed aloud, that what he had achieved was done for the sake of his own reputation, and not for that of a false lady, who could, for her sport and cold-blooded vanity, force a brave man on a duel so desperate. And, with the applause of all that were present, renounced her love for ever. This, however, was an uncommon circumstance. In general, the lady was supposed to have her lover's character as much at heart as her own, and to mean by pushing him upon enterprises of hazard give him an opportunity of meriting her good graces, which she could not with honour confer upon one undistinguished by deeds of chivalry.

Source: Essays on Chivalry, Romance, and the Drama, by Sir Walter Scott (1818)

The Evolution Of Chivalry (1818)

Influence of Women on Manners and Literature

The institution of chivalry grew chiefly out of the desire of protecting woman, exposed as she was by her weakness in those times of disorder, when society was agitated with the throes that precede the birth of establishments. As civilization advanced, and law became more strong, the original objects of the knight became by degrees almost forgotten: but the institution was too agreeable to the spirit of the age to be yet allowed to disappear. Gallantry, ambition, and a taste for martial exercises, became the chief animations of chivalry: each warrior sallied forth to maintain the peerlessness of his mistress; and Europe was covered, from one end to the other, with these adventurers; who, displaying the scarfs and crests of their ladies, knocked each other on the head to merit their favour.

However numerous the absurdities included in this custom, its influence inspired enthusiasm to poets, and gave grace and brilliancy to the nobility. Chivalry, says a German author, forms the sole glory of several centuries, which would, but for it, be consigned to horror and contempt in history. Remove from the middle ages this institution, and what would remain to them? To it we owe that extraordinary sentiment of modern times which is called *honour;* a sentiment unknown to the ancients; but which, in absence of a much higher principle, is one of the most powerful springs of noble and admired actions. Above all, it added still more to the value of the female sex in the public estimation. In the courts, in the lists, in battle, and in literature, woman was the principle source of celebration; and often the same person was at once a lover, a poet, and warrior: he could sing to his lyre, as well as combat with his lance, in behalf of the beauty by whom he had been subdued.

***

The rage for arms, however, began at length to subside. During the most flourishing times of chivalry, the most distinguished knights were but seldom able to read: as it declined, they commenced their alphabet; and when the fall of Constantinople threw the scholars of the east among the heroes of the west, learning remained no longer an unknightly accomplishment. The ladies who love not to be left behind, accordingly forsook fighting, and took to Greek. Steady, but frigid characters, slightly gifted with imagination, gave a preference to the philosophy of Aristotle; but the youthful and enthusiastic, embraced with ardour the sublime metaphysics of Plato. The fashionable manners, says a French author, were now a medly of gallantry, religion, Platonism, poetry, ancient learning, and modern theology. The women soon became distinguished by their skill and ardour in public disputation.

***

The question of the comparative rank of the two sexes was now provoked. The superiority of women was demonstrated by proofs theological, physical, cabalistical, religious, and moral. The most singular work on this subject is that of Ruscelli, which appeared in Venice in the year 1552. Moses is there made the ally of Petrarch and Dante; and the author supports his arguments by quotations from Boccacio and St. Augustine, Homer, and St. John. The ladies took an active part in this discussion, and always in their own favour. Lucretia Marinella published a book, having for title, *'The Nobility and Excellence of Women, and the Faults and Imperfections of Men;'* which certainly does not promise the fairest view of the question. Marguerite, the first wife of Henry IV, more famous for talents than for chastity, published a letter in which she undertook to prove, that *'the woman is much superior to the man.'* In 1643 there appeared at Paris, a volume entitled *'The generous woman, who shows that her sex is more economical than the other.'* But about the same time there came forth a treacherous ally of the ladies, in a work with this affronting announcement, *'The woman better than the man, a PARADOX'* by Jaques del Pozo!

We are now coming toward times when the influence of women, though not less powerful and general, bears less of the air of a new enchantment. Chivalry and scholastic philosophy seem to have been equally favourable to their celebrity. As these declined in the world; as splendid illusions of various kinds began to fade in the public view; as the affairs of mankind were put on a more practical footing; as human nature was better understood, and custom produced familiarity with almost every object of life; women lost a part of that ideal lustre which had shone around them when tournaments and colleges formed the sphere of their triumphs.

Source: The Analectic Magazine – vol XII published in Philadelphia (1818).

Instruction Of Boys In The Arts Of Chivalry (1825)

The following excerpt is from the 1825 classic The History of Chivalry Or Knighthood and Its Times, by Charles Mills. Like many historical articles it shows that chivalry came to be about much more than military conduct, becoming conflated as it were with deferent and servile behaviour toward women – as it remains to the present.

The education of a knight generally commenced at the age of seven or eight years, for no true lover of chivalry wished his children to pass their time in idleness and indulgence.

At a baronial feast, a lady in the full glow of maternal pride pointed to her offspring, and demanded of her husband whether he did not bless Heaven for having given him four such fine and promising boys. "Dame," replied her lord, thinking her observation ill timed and foolish, " so help me God and Saint Martin, nothing gives me greater sorrow and shame than to see four great sluggards, who do nothing but eat, and drink, and waste their time in idleness and folly." Like other children of gentlebirth, therefore, the boys of this noble Duke Guerin of Montglaive, in spite of their mother's wishes, commenced their chivalric exercises.

In some places there were schools appointed by the nobles of the country, but most frequently their own castles served. Every feudal lord had his court, to which he drew the sons and daughters of the poorer gentry of his domains ; and his castle was also frequented by the children of men of equal rank with himself, for (such was the modesty and courtesy of chivalry) each knight had generally some brother in arms, whom he thought better fitted than himself to grace his children with noble accomplishments.

The duties of the boy for the first seven years of his service were chiefly personal. If sometimes the harsh principles of feudal subordination gave rise to such service, it oftener proceeded from the friendly relations of life; and as in the latter case it was voluntary, there was no loss of honourable consideration in performing it. The dignity of obedience, that principle which blends the various shades of social life, and which had its origin in the patriarchal manners of early Europe, was now fostered in the castles of the feudal nobility.

The light-footed youth attended the lord and his lady in the hall, and followed them in all their exercises of war and pleasure ; and it was considered unknightly for a cavalier to wound a page in battle. He also acquired the rudiments of those incongruous subjects, religion, love, and war, so strangely blended in chivalry ; and generally the intellectual and moral education of the boy was given by the ladies of the court.

From the lips of the ladies the gentle page learned both his catechism and the art of love, and as the religion of the day was full of symbols, and addressed to the senses, so the other feature of his devotion was not to be nourished by abstract contemplation alone. He was directed to regard some one lady of the court as the type of his heart's future mistress ; she was the centre of all his hopes and wishes ; to her he was obedient, faithful, and courteous.

While the young Jean de Saintre was a page of honour at the court of the French king, the Dame des Belles Cousines enquired of him the name of the mistress of his heart's affections. The simple youth replied, that he loved his lady mother, and next to her, his sister Jacqueline was dear to him. "Young man," rejoined the lady, "I am not speaking of the affection due to your mother and sister ; but I wish to know the name of the lady to whom you are attached par amours." The poor boy was still more confused, and he could only reply, that he loved no one par amours.

The Dame des Belles Cousines charged him with being a traitor to the laws of chivalry, and declared that his craven spirit was evinced by such an avowal. " Whence," she enquired, "sprang the valiancy and knightly feats of Launcelot, Gawain, Tristram, Giron the courteous, and other ornaments of the round fable of Ponthus, and of those knights and squires of this country whom I could enumerate : whence the grandeur of many whom I have. known to arise to renown, except from the noble desire of maintaining themselves in the grace and esteem of the ladies ; without which spirit-stirring sentiment they must have ever remained in the shades of obscurity? And do you, coward valet, presume to declare that you possess no sovereign lady, and desire to have none ?"

Jean underwent a long scene of persecution on account of his confession of the want of proper chivalric sentiment, but he was at length restored to favour by the intercession of the ladies of the court. He then named as his mistress Matheline de Coucy, a child only ten years old. "Matheline is indeed a pretty girl," replied the Dame des Belles Cousines, "but what profit, what honour, what comfort, what aid, what council for advancing you in chivalrous fame can you derive from such a choice? You should elect a lady of noble blood, who has the ability to advise, and the power to assist you ; and you should serve her so truly, and love her so loyally, as to compel her to acknowledge the honourable affection which you entertain for her. For, be assured, that there is no lady, however cruel and haughty she may be, but through long service, will be induced to acknowledge and reward loyal affection with some portion of mercy.

By such a course you will gain the praise of worthy knighthood, and till then I would not give an apple for you or your achievements but he who loyally serves his lady will not only be blessed to the height of man's felicity in this life, but will never fall into those sins which will prevent his happiness hereafter. Pride will be entirely effaced until the heart of him who endeavours by humility and courtesy to win the grace of a lady. The true faith of a lover will defend him from the other deadly sins of anger, envy, sloth, and gluttony ; and his devotion to his mistress renders the thought impossible of his conduct ever being stained with the vice of incontinence."

Source: Charles Mills, The History of Chivalry Or Knighthood and Its Times (1825)

The Chivalry Fake (1913)

THE justification for the whole movement of Modern Feminism in one of its main practical aspects – namely, the placing of the female sex in the position of privilege, advantage and immunity – is concentrated in the current conception of "chivalry." It behoves us, therefore, to devote some consideration to the meaning and implication of this notion. Now this word chivalry is the *dernier ressort* of those at a loss for a justification of the modern privileging of women. But those who use it seldom give themselves the trouble to analyse the connotation of this term. Brought to book as to its meaning, most persons would probably define it as deference to, or consideration for, weakness, especially bodily weakness. Used in this sense, however, the term covers a very much wider ground than the "kow-towing" to the female section of the human race, usually associated with it. Boys, men whose muscular strength is below the average, domestic animals, etc., might all claim this special protection as a plea of chivalry, in their favour.

And yet we do not find different criminal laws, or different rules of prison treatment, say, for men whose stamina is below the average. Neither do we find such men or boys exempted by law from corporal punishment in consequence of their weakness, unless as an exception in individual cases when the weakness amounts to dangerous physical disability. Neither, again, in the general affairs of life are we accustomed to see any such deference to men of weaker muscular or constitutional development as custom exacts in the case of women. Once more, looking at the question from the other side, do we find the claim of chivalry dropped in the case of the powerful virago or the muscularly developed female athlete, the sportswoman who rides, hunts, plays cricket, football, golf and other masculine games, and who may even fence or box? Not one whit!

It would seem then that the definition of the term under consideration, based on the notion of deference to mere weakness as such, will hardly hold water, since in its application the question of sex always takes precedence of that of weakness. Let us try again! Abandoning for the moment the definition of chivalry as a consideration for weakness, considered *absolutely*, as we may term it, let us see whether the definition of consideration for *relative* defencelessness – i.e. defencelessness in a given situation – will coincide with the current usage of the word. But here again we are met with the fact that the man in the hands of the law – to wit, in the grip of the forces of the State, ay, even the strongest man, were he a very Hercules, is in as precisely as defenceless and helpless a position relative to those in whose power he finds himself, as the weakest woman would be in the like case, neither more nor less! And yet an enlightened and chivalrous public opinion tolerates the most fiendish barbarities and excogitated cruelties being perpetrated upon male convicts in our gaols, while it shudders with horror at the notion of female convicts being accorded any severity of punishment at all even for the same, or, for that matter, more heinous offences. A particularly crass and crucial illustration is that infamous piece of one-sided sex legislation which has already occupied our attention in the course of the present volume – to wit, the so-called "White Slave Traffic Act" 1912.

It is plain then that chivalry as understood in the present day really spells sex privilege and sex favouritism pure and simple, and that any attempts to define the term on a larger basis, or to give it a colourable rationality founded on fact, are simply subterfuges, conscious or unconscious, on the part of those who put them forward. The etymology of the word chivalry is well known and obvious enough. The term meant originally the virtues associated with knighthood considered as a whole, bravery even to the extent of

reckless daring, loyalty to the chief or feudal superior, generosity to
a fallen foe, general open-handedness, and open-heartedness,
including, of course, the succour of the weak and the oppressed
generally, inter alia, the female sex when in difficulties. It would be
idle, of course, to insist upon the historical definition of the term.

Language develops and words in course of time depart widely from
their original connotation, so that etymology alone is seldom of
much value in practically determining the definition of words in their
application at the present day. But the fact is none the less worthy of
note that only a fragment of the original connotation of the word
chivalry is covered by the term as used in our time, and that even
that fragment is torn from its original connection and is made to
serve as a scarecrow in the field of public opinion to intimidate all
who refuse to act upon, or who protest against, the privileges and
immunities of the female sex.[1]

I have said that even that subsidiary element in the old original
notion of chivalry which is now well-nigh the only surviving
remnant of its original connotation is torn from its connection and
hence has necessarily become radically changed in its meaning.
From being part of a general code of manners enjoined upon a
particular guild or profession it has been degraded to mean the
exclusive right in one sex guaranteed by law and custom to certain
advantages and exemptions with- out any corresponding
responsibility. Let us make no mistake about this. When the
limelight of a little plain but critical common-sense is turned upon
this notion of chivalry hitherto regarded as so sacrosanct, it is seen to
be but a poor thing after all; and when men have acquired the habit
of habitually turning the light of such criticism upon it, the
accusation, so terrible in the present state of public opinion, of being
"unchivalrous" will lose its terrors for them.

In the so-called ages of chivalry themselves it never meant, as it does
today, the woman right or wrong. It never meant as it does today the
general legal and social privilege of sex. It never meant a social
defence or a legal exoneration for the bad and even the criminal
woman, simply because she is a woman. It meant none of these
things. All it meant was a voluntary or gratuitous personal service to
the forlorn women which the members of the Knights' guild among

other such services, many of them taking precedence of this one, were supposed to perform.

So far as courage is concerned, which was perhaps the first of the chivalric virtues in the old days, it certainly requires more courage in our days to deal severely with a woman when she deserves it (as a man would be dealt with in like circumstances) than it does to back up a woman against her wicked male opponent.

It is a cheap thing, for example, in the case of a man and woman quarrelling in the street, to play out the stage rôle of the bold and gallant Englishman "who won't see a woman maltreated and put upon, not he!" and this, of course, without any inquiry into the merits of the quarrel. To swim with the stream, to make a pretence of boldness and bravery, when all the time you know you have the backing of conventional public opinion and mob-force behind you, is the cheapest of mock heroics.

Chivalry to-day means the woman, right or wrong, just as patriotism to-day means "my country right or wrong." In other words, chivalry to-day is only another name for Sentimental Feminism. Every outrageous pretension Of Sentimental Feminism can be justified by the appeal to chivalry, which amounts (to use the German expression) to an appeal from Pontius to Pilate. This Sentimental Feminism commonly called chivalry is sometimes impudently dubbed by its votaries, "manliness." It will presumably continue in its practical effects until a sufficient minority of sensible men will have the moral courage to beard a Feminist public opinion and shed a little of this sort of "manliness." The plucky Welshmen at Llandystwmdwy in their dealings with the suffragette rowdies on memorable occasion showed themselves capable of doing this. In fact one good effect generally of militant suffragetteism seems to be the weakening of the notion of chivalry – i.e. in its modern sense of Sentimental Feminism – amongst the populace of this country.

The combination of Sentimental Feminism with its invocation of the old-world sentiment of chivalry which was based essentially on the assumption of the mental, moral and physical inferiority of woman to man, for its justification, with the pretensions of modern Political Feminism, is simply grotesque in its inconsistent absurdity. In this way Modern Feminism would fain achieve the feat of eating its cake and having it too. When political and economic rights are in question, *bien entendu*, such as involve gain and social standing, the assumption of inferiority magically disappears before the strident assertion of the dogma of the equality of woman with man – her mental and moral equality certainly! When, however, the question is of a different character – for example, for the relieving of some vile female criminal of the penalty of her misdeeds-then Sentimental Feminism comes into play, then the whole *plaidoyer* is based on the chivalric sentiment of deference and consideration for poor, weak woman. I may point out that here, if it be in the least degree logical, the plea for mercy or immunity can hardly be based on any other consideration than that of an intrinsic moral weakness in view of which the offence is to be condoned.

The plea of physical weakness, if such be entertained, is here in most cases purely irrelevant. Thus, as regards the commutation of the death sentence, the question of the muscular strength or weakness of the condemned person does not come in at all. The same applies, *mutatis mutandis*, to many other forms of criminal punishment. But it must not be forgotten that there are two aspects of physical strength or weakness. There is, as we have already pointed out, the muscular aspect and the constitutional aspect. If we concede the female sex as essentially and inherently weaker in muscular power and development than the male, this by no means involves the assumption that woman is constitutionally weaker than man. On the contrary, it is a known fact attested, as far as I am aware, by all physiologists, no less than by common observation, that the constitutional toughness and power of endurance of woman in general far exceeds that of man, as explained in an earlier chapter. This resilient power of the system, its capacity for enduring strain, it may here be remarked in passing, is by no means necessarily a characteristic of a specially high stage of organic evolution. We find it indeed in many orders of invertebrate animals in striking forms. Be this as it may, however, the existence of this greater constitutional strength or resistant power in the female than in the male organic system – as crucially instanced by the markedly greater death-rate of boys than of girls in infancy and early childhood – should, in respect of severity of punishment, prison treatment, etc., be a strong counterargument against the plea for leniency, or immunity in the case of female criminals, made by the advocates of Sentimental Feminism.

But these considerations afford only one more illustration of the utter irrationality of the whole movement of Sentimental Feminism identified with the notion of "chivalry." For the rest, we may find illustrations of this galore. A very flagrant case is that infamous "rule of the sea" which came so much into prominence at the time of the *Titanic* disaster. Recording to this preposterous "chivalric" Feminism, in the case of a ship foundering, it is the unwritten law of the seas, not that the passengers shall leave the ship and be rescued in their order as they come, but that the whole female portion shall have the right of being rescued before any man is allowed to leave the ship. Now this abominable piece of sex favouritism, on the face of it, cries aloud in its irrational injustice. Here is no question of bodily strength or weakness, either muscular or constitutional. In this respect, for the nonce, all are on a level. But it is a case of life itself. A number of poor wretches are doomed to a watery grave, simply and solely because they have not had the luck to be born of the privileged female sex.

Such is "chivalry" as understood to-day – the deprivation, the robbery from men of the most elementary personal rights in order to endow women with privileges at the expense of men. During the ages of chivalry and for long after it was not so. Law and custom then was the same for men as for women in its incidence. To quote the familiar proverb in a slightly altered form, *then* – "what was sauce for the gander was sauce for the goose." Not until the nineteenth century did this state of things change. Then for the first time the law began to respect persons and to distinguish in favour of sex.

Even taking the matter on the conventional ground of weakness and granting, for the sake of argument, the relative muscular weakness of the female as ground for her being allowed the immunity claimed by Modern Feminists of the sentimental school, the distinction is altogether lost sight of between weakness as such and *aggressive* weakness. Now I submit there is a very considerable difference between what is due to weakness that is harmless and unprovocative, and weakness that is *aggressive*, still more when this aggressive weakness presumes on itself as weakness, and on the consideration extended to it, in order to become tyrannical and oppressive. Weakness as such assuredly deserves all consideration, but aggressive weakness deserves none save to be crushed beneath the iron heel of strength. Woman at the present day has been encouraged by a Feminist public opinion to become meanly aggressive under the protection of her weakness. She has been encouraged to forge her gift of weakness into a weapon of tyranny against man, unwitting that in so doing she has deprived her weakness of all just claim to consideration or even to toleration.

Footnote:

1. One among many apposite cases, which has occurred recently, was protested against in a letter to *The Daily Telegraph*, 21st March 1913, in which it was pointed out that while a suffragette got a few months' imprisonment in the second division for wilfully setting fire to the pavilion in Kew Gardens, a few days previously, at the Lewes Assizes, a man had been sentenced to five years' penal servitude for burning a rick!!

Source: Ernest B. Bax, *The Fraud of Feminism* (1913)

The Dream Of Heroism And Love (1924)

The knight and his lady, that is to say, the hero who serves for love, this is the primary and invariable motif from which erotic fantasy will always start. It is sensuality transformed into the craving for self-sacrifice, into the desire of the male to show his courage, to incur danger, to be strong, to suffer and to bleed before his lady-love.

From the moment when the dream of heroism through love has intoxicated the yearning heart, fantasy grows and overflows. The first simple theme is soon left behind, the soul thirsts for new fancies, and passion colours the dream of suffering and of renunciation. The man will not be content merely to suffer, he will want to save from danger, or from suffering, the object of his desire. A more vehement stimulus is added to the primary motif: its chief feature will be that of defending imperilled virginity—in other words, that of ousting the rival. This, then, is the essential theme of chivalrous love poetry : the young hero, delivering the virgin. The sexual motif is always behind it, even when the aggressor is only an artless dragon; a glance at Burne-Jones's famous picture suffices to prove it.

One is surprised that comparative mythology should have looked so indefatigably to meteorological phenomena for the explanation of such an immediate and perpetual motif as the deliverance of the virgin, which is the oldest of literary motifs, and one which can never grow antiquated. It may from time to time become stale from over-much repetition, and yet it will reappear, adapting itself to all times and surroundings. New romantic types will arise, just as the cowboy has succeeded the corsair.

***

Nowhere does the erotic element of the tournament appear more clearly than in the custom of the knight's wearing the veil or the dress of his lady. In Perceforest we read how the lady spectators of the combat take off their finery, one article after another, to throw them to the knights in the lists. At the end of the fight they are bareheaded and without sleeves. A poem of the thirteenth century, the work of a Picard or a Hainault minstrel, entitled Des trois Chevaliers et del Chainse,[1] has worked out this motif in all its force. The wife of a nobleman of great liberality, but not very fond of fighting, sends her shirt to three knights who serve her for love, that one of them at the tournament which her husband is going to give may wear it as a coat-armour, without any mail underneath. The first and the second knights excuse themselves. The third, who is poor, takes the shirt in his arms at night, and kisses it passionately. He appears at the tournament, dressed in the shirt and without a coat of mail; he is grievously wounded, the shirt, stained with his blood, is torn. Then his extraordinary bravery is perceived and he is awarded the prize. The lady gives him her heart. The lover asks something in his turn. He sends back the garment, all blood-stained, to the lady, that she may wear it over her gown at the meal which is to conclude the feast. She embraces it tenderly and shows herself dressed in the shirt as the knight had demanded. The majority of those present blame her, the husband is confounded, and the minstrel winds up by asking the question : Which of the two lovers sacrificed most for the sake of the other?

***

The warlike sports of the Middle Ages differ from Greek and modern athletics by being far less simple and natural. Pride, honour, love and art give additional stimulus to the competition itself. Overloaded with pomp and decoration, full of heroic fancy, they serve to express romantic needs too strong for mere literature to satisfy. The realities of court life or a military career offered too little opportunity for the fine make-belief of heroism and love, which filled the soul. So they had to be acted. The staging of the tournament, therefore, had to be that of romance ; that is to say, the imaginary world of Arthur, where the fancy of a fairy-tale was enhanced by the sentimentality of courtly love.

Note: [1] Of the three knights and the shirt.